Sandlands

The Suffolk Coast and Heaths

Tom Williamson

WIND*gather*
PRESS

Published by: Windgather Press Ltd, 29 Bishop Road, Bollington, Macclesfield, Cheshire SK10 5NX, UK

Distributed by: Central Books Ltd, 99 Wallis Road, London E9 5LN, UK

British Library Cataloguing-in-Publication Data
A catalogue record for this book is available from the British Library

ISBN 10: 1-905119-02-X
ISBN 13: 978-1-905119-02-8

Designed, typeset and originated by
Carnegie Publishing Ltd, Chatsworth Road, Lancaster
Printed and bound by
Cambridge University Press

L942·64

SANDLANDS

Contents

List of Figures

Abbreviations

IRO   Suffolk Record Office (Ipswich)
LRO   Suffolk Record Office (Lowestoft)
TNA: PRO   The National Archives: Public Record Office

Acknowledgements

....

A great deal of the research for this book was carried out by Ivan Ringwood and Sarah Harrison, both meticulous researchers with an enviable ability to ferret out useful and interesting nuggets of information. Their work, and much of mine, was generously funded at various times by the Suffolk Coast and Heaths AONB, English Heritage, Suffolk County Council and the Sutton Hoo Society. I have also drawn extensively on the work of past research students at the University of East Anglia, especially that of Richard Farrand, Gudrum Reinke, Rosemary Hoppitt and Margaret Thomas. Phillip Judge drew the maps and diagrams, with his customary good grace; Malcolm Farrow supplied the photographs for figures 2, 3, 10, 13, 14, 17, 23, 32, 43, 45, 46, 49, 50, 68, 69 and 72; Cliff Hoppitt provided figure 9; and Gary Battell provided figure 48. The aerial photographs in figures 6, 15, 63 and 70 are by Damian Grady and are reproduced with permission of English Heritage. The research of other people into the history and archaeology of this part of Suffolk has provided both inspiration and information, and I owe in particular a great debt to E. Burrell, whose MA dissertation on the *Historical Geography of the Sandlings*, written in 1960, remains the most important work on the district; to Peter Warner; to Norman Scarfe; and to Cain Hegarty and Sarah Newsome, who provided me with important information from their recent study of the Suffolk inter-tidal zone, funded by English Heritage as part of the National Mapping Programme. Thanks also to the staff of the Lowestoft Record Office and the Ipswich Record Office for their help and advice, and to the latter for permission to reproduce figures 7, 27, 33 and 36; figure 61 is reproduced with permission of the Orford Town Trust. Edward Martin, Simon Hooton and Peter Holborn all provided invaluable comments on the initial report from which this short volume has grown. Lastly, I would like to thank my family – Liz Bellamy, Matt Williamson and Jess Williamson – for their usual tolerance of my obsessive interest in all things connected with the landscape.

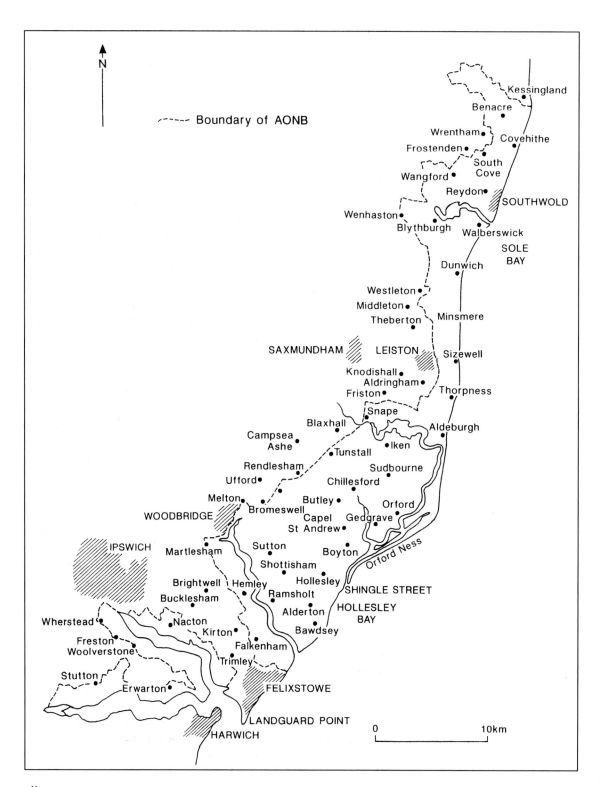

N

- - - - Boundary of AONB

Kessingland
Benacre
Wrentham
Covehithe
Frostenden
South Cove
Wangford
Reydon
SOUTHWOLD
Wenhaston
Blythburgh
Walberswick
SOLE BAY
Dunwich
Westleton
Middleton
Theberton
Minsmere
SAXMUNDHAM
LEISTON
Sizewell
Knodishall
Aldringham
Friston
Thorpness
Snape
Blaxhall
Aldeburgh
Campsea Ashe
Iken
Tunstall
Rendlesham
Sudbourne
Ufford
Chillesford
Melton
Butley
Orford
Bromeswell
Capel St Andrew
Gedgrave
WOODBRIDGE
IPSWICH
Martlesham
Sutton
Boyton
Orford Ness
Shottisham
Brightwell
Hemley
Hollesley
SHINGLE STREET
Bucklesham
Ramsholt
HOLLESLEY BAY
Wherstead
Nacton
Alderton
Freston
Kirton
Bawdsey
Woolverstone
Falkenham
Stutton
Trimley
Erwarton
FELIXSTOWE
LANDGUARD POINT
HARWICH

0   10km

xii

CHAPTER ONE

History and Environment

....

Introducing the Sandlings

This book is about the making of a unique landscape, that of the narrow strip of countryside that runs down the east coast of Suffolk, between the claylands and the sea. This is a low-lying yet gently rolling area, surprisingly un-developed and uncommercialised, with only a handful of genteel historic towns but many scattered hamlets and villages. It is a remote, secluded world of quiet woodland, lonely heaths and extensive coastal wetlands, rich in birdlife. The district's unspoilt and distinctive character led to its designation in 1969 as an 'Area of Outstanding Natural Beauty' (AONB), called 'Suffolk Coast and Heaths'. Most of this distinctive area has, however, long had its own name: the *Sandlings*, or *Sandlands* (Figure 1).

The coast itself is perhaps the district's most immediately striking element. Estuaries are prominent and contain areas of unreclaimed salt marsh and drained grazing marsh, as well as extensive mudflats (Figure 2) (Land Use Consultants 1993, 14–17). Several have been completely sealed off from the sea by the development of shingle banks, and comprise self-contained landscapes of reed beds and pasture bounded by rising, often wooded, ground. However, the majority of the district consists of a low, sandy plateau, mainly lying at between twenty metres and thirty metres OD and seldom rising to more than fifty metres above sea level. Parts of this plateau are still occupied by heath, with wide expanses of heather and grassland together with areas of gorse, broom and birch (Figure 3). Yet large tracts consist of farmland, mainly under arable crops but with some extensive pig-farming. Monotonous, featureless prairies can be found, as in other parts of East Anglia, but usually there is a strong visual framework of hedges, hedgerow trees, and woods (Land Use Consultants 1993, 22–3). In many places extensive woodlands dominate the landscape: particularly striking are the conifer plantations established in the first half of the twentieth century by the Forestry Commission.

The special qualities and distinctive character of this district have long been recognised. The anonymous author of the *Chorography of Suffolk*, written in *c.* 1605, divided the county into three principal districts: 'Woodlande & High Suffolcke', corresponding with the band of heavy boulder clay running through the centre; an area in the north-west, which we today call Breckland, which he described as 'mostly heathy and barren and fit only for sheepe and

I

FIGURE 2.
Typical Sandlings
scenery: a view across
arable fields towards
the great inland estuary
of the Alde and Ore.

conyes'; and this strip of land running along the coast, which he considered 'fitte for sheep and corne' (MacCulloch 1976, 19). Just over a century later, in 1735, John Kirby employed the same tripartite division but used the term 'Sandlands' for the coastal district which extended 'from Landguard Fort to Yarmouth' (Kirby 1735, 1–2). Kirby, and almost all subsequent writers, thus excluded from the Sandlings the area of the Shotley peninsula in the extreme south, which has very different soils – more fertile loams, derived from light brickearth overlying gravels. Although much of the Shotley peninsula is included within the Coast and Heaths AONB it was never really part of the Sandlings in the strict sense, which begins on the northern side of the Orwell estuary. The area will be discussed to some extent in this book, but for the most part our attention will focus on the Sandlings proper.

The character of landscape: soils, topography, and location

In spite of the area's designation as an Area of Outstanding Natural Beauty, there is little in the landscape of the Coast and Heaths which could be described in any meaningful sense as 'natural', with the exception of the shore-line itself. Heaths, marshes and woodlands, as much as arable farmland, were created by human activity: the structure and appearance of the countryside was

shaped, over a very long period of time, by social and economic forces. But
these forces operated on, and within, a natural framework, and it is to this
which we must first turn (Figure 4).

The most important influences on any landscape are geology and soils, and
the essential feature of the Sandlings is the contrast between the acid, sandy
soils that characterise most of the higher ground, and the extensive tracts of
peat and alluvium found at, or below, sea level. The solid geology of the
uplands is, for the most part, characterised by the formation known as *crag* –
a complex sequence of shelly sands, gravels and clays laid down in late Pliocene
and early Pleistocene times (between *c.* 3.5 and 1.6 million years ago) with, at
its base, a detritus bed containing nodules rich in lime phosphates (Chatwin
1961). Further south, these formations are replaced by the earlier London clay,
while in the area around Westleton and Dunwich the sandy and gravelly beds
called the Westleton Beds were laid down on the margins of a sea that retreated
after the crag was formed. All these deposits have had an important, if sometimes subtle, effect upon the landscape, providing building stone, material for
improving the quality of the surface soil, and the raw material for a local
nineteenth-century coprolite industry. For the most part, however, they are

FIGURE 3.
Dunwich: the
combination of open
heathland, cliffs and sea
gives the Sandlings
landscape much of its
distinctive character.

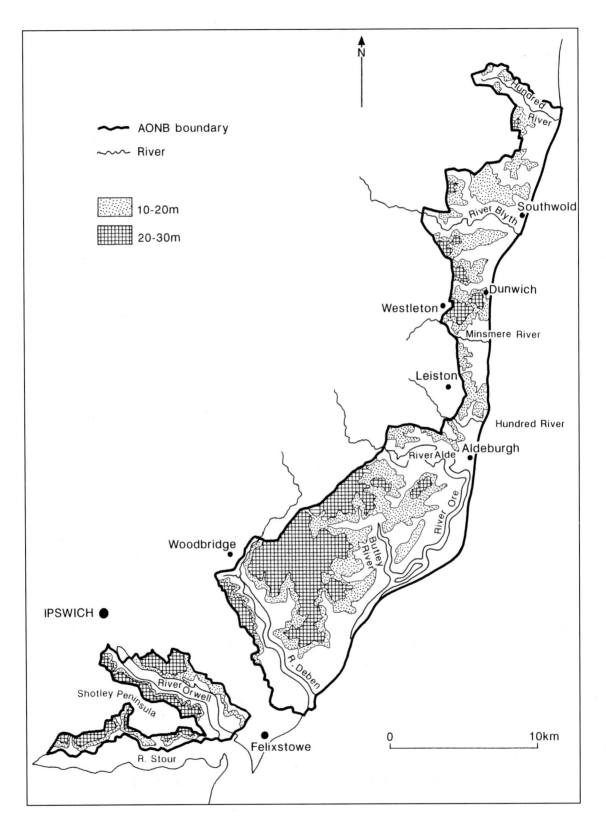

N

AONB boundary
River

10-20m
20-30m

Hundred River

Southwold

River Blyth

Dunwich

Westleton

Minsmere River

Leiston

Hundred River

Aldeburgh

River Alde

River Ore

Butley River

Woodbridge

IPSWICH

R. Deben

Shotley Peninsula

River Orwell

R. Stour

Felixstowe

0   10km

obscured by rather more recent layers of glacial sand and gravel – a complex and varied range of materials left by streams running out from the same ice sheet that deposited the more extensive areas of boulder clay which are found immediately to the west of the district, occupying the central part of the county, known as 'High' Suffolk (Wymer 1999). These sands and gravels have a thickness of thirty metres in places, but average around ten metres. They give rise to the acid, sandy soils which are, and have always been, the district's most notable characteristic; so too do most of the earlier formations, which are sporadically exposed on the surface, especially the Westleton Beds near Dunwich. But some of the Crag deposits – the Coralline Crag and the Red Crag – contain a high proportion of shells and where these deposits outcrop more calcareous soils occur, although these remain very dry and porous.

Although the term 'Sandlings' or 'Sandlands' was generally used to describe the whole of the sandy coastal strip of Suffolk north of the Orwell estuary, it was sometimes more narrowly employed. Arthur Young, writing in 1797, noted that while the soils of the whole coastal district were formed in sand, the term 'Sandlings' was 'given peculiarly to the country south of the line of Woodbridge and Orford, where a large extent of poor, and even blowing sands is found' (Young 1797). Further north, the soils were often more loamy and more profitable to farm, so that 'there are few districts in the county, if any, abounding with wealthier farmers'. This distinction between the north and south of the district is strongly echoed in modern soil maps (Figure 5). South of Aldeburgh, soils of the Newport 4 Association are dominant. These are deep and well-drained, but acid and very infertile, sandy and stony soils which are formed in fluvio-glacial deposits (Hodge *et al.* 1984, 277–8). They are interdigitated with areas of the slightly less infertile and acidic soils of the Newport 2 Association, which generally occur on lower ground and are formed in deposits of the underlying crag as well as in glacial sands (Hodge *et al.* 1984, 272–3). To the north of Aldeburgh, in contrast, while Newport 4 soils again cover extensive areas (especially in the area immediately to the south of Walberswick) there are also large tracts of Newport 3 Association soils. These are loamy as well as sandy, being formed in both fluvio-glacial sands and in patches of boulder clay and 'head' (i.e., glacially redeposited clay material) (Hodge *et al.* 1984, 274–7).

There are other important differences in soils and topography between the north and the south of the district, differences which have been crucial in the history of agriculture and settlement. To the south of Aldeburgh the sandy coastal strip is generally wider than to the north, reaching its greatest extent in the area around Rendlesham Forest, where the distance between the clay plateau to the west and the marshes to the east exceeds ten kilometres. North of Aldeburgh, in contrast, the sands are seldom more than five kilometres in width, and often less than three. The boundaries of the modern AONB reflect this fact, embracing a much wider tract of territory to the south than to the north. This pattern of soils and geology ensures that, while parishes in the south of the district – such as Orford, Sutton, Alderton or Shottisham – generally

FIGURE 4.
The Sandlings, showing relief and some of the principal topographic features mentioned in the text.

FIGURE 5.
overleaf left
The Sandlings, showing the distribution of the principal soil types.

FIGURE 6.
overleaf right
An aerial panorama of the coastal landscape between Aldeburgh and Minsmere. In the middle distance is the early twentieth-century holiday village of Thorpness, set around The Meare, a modified natural water body which formed in the lee of the shingle spit. Beyond is the heathland of Aldringham Common, and surrounding woodland of nineteenth-century date. In the distance are the domes of Sizewell nuclear power station, with the reedbeds of Minsmere, another blocked estuary, beyond.

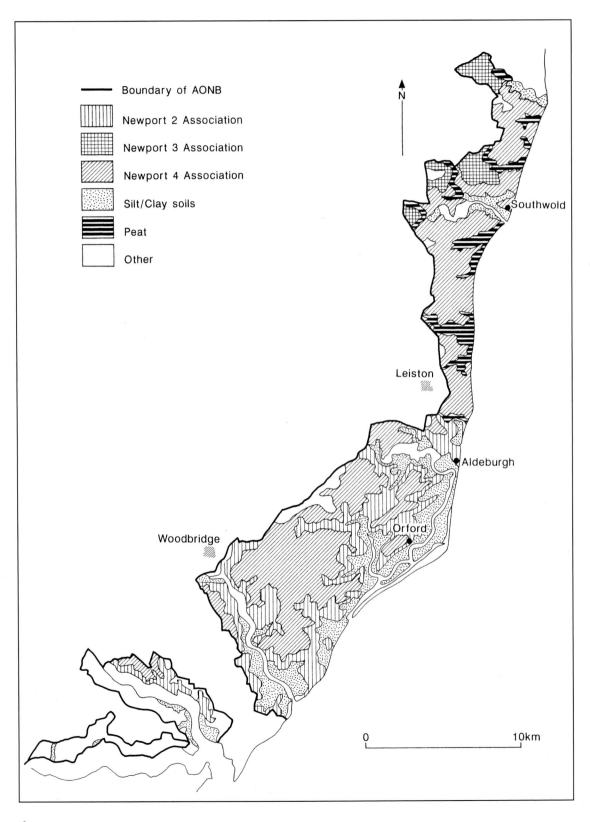

Boundary of AONB

Newport 2 Association

Newport 3 Association

Newport 4 Association

Silt/Clay soils

Peat

Other

N

Southwold

Leiston

Aldeburgh

Orford

Woodbridge

0   10km

extend *only* over sands and coastal marshes, many of those located to the north run up on to the heavier but more fertile soils of the boulder clays to the west.

The character of the coastal wetlands in the areas lying to the north and south of Aldeburgh is also rather different. In the north, most of the low ground comprises estuaries of relatively minor watercourses which have been entirely blocked by shingle spits, formed by the process known as 'longshore drift' and by periodic north-easterly gales. The streams and rivers reach the sea by passing through these banks of material, and their valleys are thus poorly-drained and are largely filled with deposits of peat, which formed in lagoons of fresh water. These areas often remained as unreclaimed fen until well into the post-medieval period (Figure 6). To the south, in contrast, the majority of low land consists of silt/clay alluvial deposits, formed behind more extensive spits associated with larger rivers – the Deben and the Alde. Originally tidal salt marsh, much of this land was, from early medieval times, improved by 'inning' or embanking. Peaty soils are here largely restricted to a narrow strip at the edge of the marshes. In these various ways, the soils and topography of the north and the south of the Sandlings differ considerably one from another, and these differences have had a major effect on the development of their respective landscapes over the long centuries.

Soils and topography affected the development of the landscape in innumerable and complex ways, as we shall see. But the personality of any region, and the character of its landscape, does not arise solely from soils, topography or other immediate aspects of the natural environment. Patterns of contact with other places, and the styles and ideas that such contacts brought, were also of crucial importance in moulding local and regional identity. Here the Sandlings' most important feature was the ease of communication provided by the sea, and the open, inviting nature of its coast, which had few significant offshore shoals or sandbanks, and numerous safe moorings in sheltered havens and estuaries. In these respects the Suffolk coast differs somewhat from that of Essex, to the south of the Stour estuary, where shoals and mudflats have always provided a less appealing landfall. In spite of its long shoreline, the county of Essex has never had as strong a maritime tradition as its northern neighbour. Indeed, the northern stretch of the Essex coast represents in many ways a cut-off point in patterns of contact and communication. Trade, invaders and cultural influences coming down the east coast, or across the North Sea, tend to peter out when the mouth of the Stour is reached and Essex's contacts, like those of south-west Suffolk, have always mainly been with the south-east of England, London, and northern France. The Sandlings, in contrast, has looked more to the north, towards Scandinavia, north Germany and the Low Countries, and like the rest of north-east Suffolk has always had more in common with Norfolk than with the south and west of the county. Again and again this pattern of allegiance is reflected in archaeological distributions and cultural patterns: in the distribution of Scandinavian place names; in the use of the distinctive, wavy 'pantiles' as a roofing material; in such characteristic aspects of the ecclesiastical heritage as round church towers, or the habit of building two churches in a single, or in adjacent, churchyards. In the Iron Age the Sandlings and north-east Suffolk were occupied by the Iceni; Essex and south-west Suffolk were Trinovantian territory and enjoyed close trading contacts with the Roman world (Haselgrove 1982; Cunliffe 1995, 58–97). In early Anglo-Saxon times, after the collapse of Roman rule in Britain, Sandlings people both inhumed and cremated their dead, again like those living in areas to the north. But those in south-west Suffolk and Essex, in common with those throughout south-east England, practiced inhumation alone, or followed some rite of disposal which has left no obvious trace in the archaeological record (Lucy 2000, 140–5). The Lark-Gipping corridor (roughly speaking, a line running from Bury St Edmunds to Ipswich) has long been a fundamental cultural barrier dividing East Anglia in two, and the Sandlings has always stood firmly to the north and east of that line.

Yet the sea was more than a conduit for people, goods and influences. It has always had a more direct impact on the development of the landscape. Patterns of erosion and deposition created the marshes and fens which are such a key feature of the scenery; trade and fishing allowed the development of important ports; in more recent times, beaches and the sea have encouraged some limited development of holiday resorts. Above all, a coastline open to foreign influences, welcoming to ships and boats, was also one that was inviting to attackers and invaders, and so the needs of national defence have left an indelible mark upon the local landscape. In short, the wide and restless sea has, in innumerable ways, moulded the history of the Sandlings.

The earliest settlers

The light, easily-worked soils of the Sandlings encouraged settlement from an early date. Before the later Iron Age, farmers used a simple breaking-plough or *ard*, without a coulter or mouldboard. The cultivation of heavy loam or clay soils was difficult with such an implement and, although early prehistoric settlement was certainly more widespread than an earlier generation of archaeologists believed, the most densely-settled districts do seem to have been those of light, porous soils, formed in chalk or sand. In Suffolk, the core areas of prehistoric settlement were thus the Breckland in the north-west of the county, and the Sandlings, especially the southern Sandlings – the area around Martlesham Heath and Foxhall, which formed part of a wider zone of light soil extending southwards into Essex. It is in these districts, rather than on the central claylands of the county, that the majority of Bronze Age round barrows – and the 'ring ditches' which appear on aerial photographs where these monuments have been levelled by ploughing – are located (Martin 1999b; Lawson *et al.* 1981).

In part this distribution reflects patterns of survival and recovery. Large areas of land in these light land districts remained unploughed, or only sporadically cultivated, in the Middle Ages and after, being occupied by sheep-walks and heathland. Early prehistoric monuments were thus more likely to survive here than in places where later arable land use was intensive. More importantly, aerial photography works much better on these light, freely-draining soils than it does on the clays of central Suffolk. Even allowing for this, however, there is little doubt that monuments like these were always more common on the sands, while aerial reconnaissance has shown that a number of major ceremonial centres were established here in Neolithic and Bronze Age times – like the 'causewayed enclosure' of Neolithic date located by aerial photography at Freston, overlooking the river Orwell (TM 168379) (Hegarty and Newsome 2005, 21–3).

It is possible that much larger numbers of round barrows survived in the area until relatively recently. John Norden's maps of the Stanhope estates, surveyed in 1600–01, shows numerous mound-like features on the heaths and sheepwalks, usually clustered in small groups. While it is possible that this symbol merely denotes rough or hilly ground it is noteworthy that it is used to denote the burial mounds which still survive at Sutton Hoo, and others which have only been levelled in relatively recent years, in Wantisden and Bromeswell (Figure 7) (IRO V5/22/1; EE5/11/1). In all, more than sixteen groups of mounds are depicted, all in plausible topographical locations for early barrows. If they were indeed barrows, then they were presumably levelled as periodic ploughing of the heaths intensified in the course of the seventeenth century, and as large-scale reclamations were made in the eighteenth and nine-teenth. Barrows not only stood in the way of the plough: they also comprised useful reservoirs of topsoil which could be spread on the adjacent fields.

Although the Sandlings was evidently a well-peopled district in relative terms, it is difficult to quantify the actual intensity of settlement in the Neolithic and Bronze Age. This is because settlements of this date leave fairly ephemeral traces. Those of the Neolithic period, in particular, are usually represented only by small numbers of pits containing pottery and other refuse – like those excavated at Sutton Hoo or Martlesham (Martin 1993, 49). Many of the known Bronze Age settlements were, in fact, discovered during the exca-vation of barrows which had been erected over them, as at Martlesham Heath and Brightwell Heath. The most completely excavated early prehistoric site is that at Sutton Hoo. Here, a small early Bronze Age settlement comprised a group of round houses, the best preserved of which (under Mound 2 of the Anglo-Saxon cemetery) consisted of a ring of upright timbers, each up to 300 mm in diameter, which was presumably infilled with wattle and daub and surmounted by a thatched roof. The houses were set in substantial ditched enclosures, each covering up to a hectare (Carver 1998, 97).

For the Iron Age – conventionally defined as the period running from *c.* 750 BC to the time of the Roman Conquest in AD 43 – it is possible to gain a rather clearer impression of both the numbers and the distribution of settlements. Fairly large quantities of reasonably durable pottery were in use in the district in this period, and so a high proportion of settlement sites can be discovered through field-walking surveys. In the valleys of the rivers Deben and Fynn, Iron Age settlements – mostly undefended single farmsteads – are scattered at

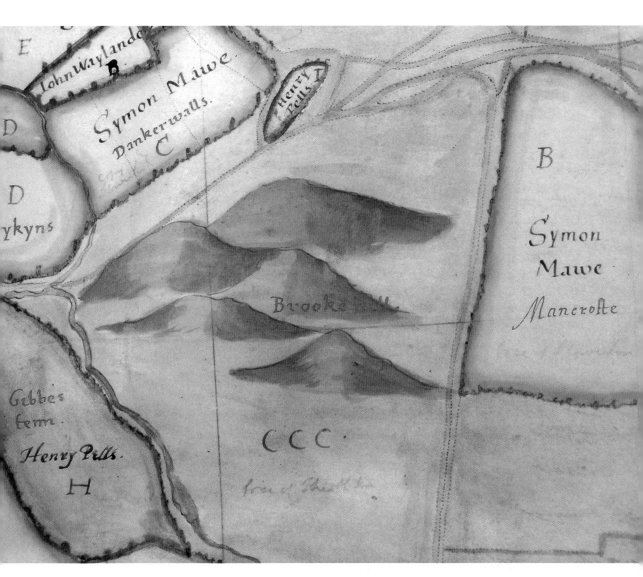

Within the map, the following hand-written labels appear:

E

John Wayland B

Symon Mawe

Dankerwalls

C

Henry Pells

D

D

ykyns

B

Symon

Mawe

Mancrofte

Brooke hill

Gibbes fenn.

Henry Pells.

H

CCC.

FIGURE 7.
An extract from John Norden's survey of the Stanhope estates, made in 1600–01, showing what may be round barrows on the heaths in Bromeswell, since levelled.

fairly regular intervals of between 700 m and 1 km (Martin 1993; 1999a). They are mainly located within 500 m of the rivers, at around 30 m OD. At least one larger settlement site existed in the area – at Burgh-by-Woodbridge, a few kilometres outside the AONB. This consisted of a defensive site of 'hill fort' type covering an area of around seven hectares, encircled by double ditches and banks (Martin 1988), and may have been a regional tribal centre with, in part, a religious or ceremonial function. It has been suggested that it originally served some section of the Iceni tribe, and was later annexed by people of Trinovantian/Catauvellaunian affiliation from the south, for the excavation recovered a clear phase of destruction, after which pottery of the type found further to the south, in Essex, came into use. The 'fort', lying on the south-western fringes of the Sandlings, probably stood close to the boundary of Icenian territory.

In spite of their wild and natural appearance, the heaths which still form such an important component of the Sandlings landscape were created by human activity. The land in these areas was originally occupied by woodland of oak and birch but, following deforestation, soil deterioration occurred, leading in time to the development of the extremely acid and infertile soils that characterise the area today (Dimbleby 1962). What remains uncertain is when this occurred, how rapidly, and to what extent the process of clearance may have been reversed on occasions, with woodland returning to formerly deforested ground. It is often suggested that heaths were created by very early clearances – in the Neolithic and Bronze Age – and have remained free of woodland ever since – or at least, until recent changes in farming practice. But it is likely that in the Sandlings heathland formation was a gradual process which was reversed to varying extents in subsequent periods. At Sutton Hoo the inhabitants of the early Bronze Age settlement cultivated barley, oats and wheat on soils which must have been at least moderately fertile. Moreover, the area was not yet completely deforested, for they also had access to hazelnuts and oak trees. The excavator of the site suggested that 'the early Bronze Age landscape may be envisaged as an open park-like countryside with mature oak trees ...' (Carver 1998, 98). During the middle Bronze Age the settlement was abandoned and cultivation ceased. Sheep, or possibly cattle, were now folded in large enclosures which were constructed of upright poles some 200 mm in diameter. But in the middle Iron Age, from about 500 BC, arable land use was resumed and a planned 'co-axial' field system was laid out across the site. The fields were cross-ploughed with a light ard, and cultivation continued here well into the Roman period (Carver 1998, 98–9). It was only then that the soils deteriorated rapidly, leading in time to the abandonment of arable farming on the site. The landscape became one of rough acid grass, growing in almost pure sand, with only a light scatter of trees – hazel, oak, and beech (Carver 1998, 100).

Here, as elsewhere, the Roman Conquest initially brought few changes to the agrarian economy, although the density of settlement may have increased. Field-walking surveys carried out by the archaeologist John Newman have revealed 'numerous scatters of greyware pottery sherds which probably indicate the locations of small farm sites' (Newman 1992, 30). Newman's meticulous survey revealed an average density of around one such site in every two square kilometres, although not all were necessarily in use at the same time. Many occupied the sites of earlier Iron Age settlements. The impression is of a settled, cleared landscape. Yet it is noteworthy that the density of settlements is rather less than in the areas of boulder clay to the west of the Sandlings, which were now being opened up for settlement and cultivation on a large scale. Here settlement densities, at least in and around the major valleys, were around twice those on the sands, at around one site per square kilometre (Hardy and Martin 1986; Hardy and Martin 1987). The improved ploughs which had been developed during the later Iron Age now allowed these more difficult, but more fertile, soils to be brought into cultivation.

The Romano-British settlement pattern did not consist only of individual farmsteads. Larger settlements – villages, or small towns – existed near Knodishall, and at Walton, near Felixstowe. The latter was associated with one of the 'Saxon Shore' forts which were built along the south and east coast in the later third century, probably to protect the coast from barbarian raiding (although possibly as part of an attempt to control trade and levy customs duties more effectively (Cotterill 1993)). The fort was washed into the sea in the seventeenth century, leaving no trace, and debate continues over whether surviving drawings of the site are genuine, or antiquarian forgeries (Fairclough and Plunkett 2000).

Metal-detecting surveys carried out on the scattered Roman farms in the district suggest that there was a serious economic, and perhaps demographic, decline in the later fourth century. Finds of late Roman coins are much less frequent than those from the early Roman period, suggesting that sites were either being abandoned altogether or were no longer integrated with a wider market economy (Newman 1992, 32). Any decline in the wealth and numbers of settlements on these light soils, however, was minor compared with that on the claylands to the west, where large-scale abandonment of land seems to have taken place in the late Roman period, especially on the most level and poorly-drained areas. By the time that Anglo-Saxon immigrants began to arrive in the fifth century, settlement in Suffolk was once again strongly concentrated on the light soils, in the Sandlings and Breckland, in what was effectively a return to the distribution patterns of early prehistory. This change may reflect a measure of technological regression as well as demographic decline.

The Anglian legacy

There is little doubt that the Sandlings district formed, from the fifth into the eighth century, one of the most important centres of political power in England. The district, and especially its southern portions, is littered with sites of considerable early and middle Saxon importance (Figure 8), and almost certainly formed the heartland from which the dynasty called the *Wuffingas* came to rule the whole of East Anglia. The most famous of these sites is, of course, the cemetery at Sutton Hoo: a collection of burials, many under barrows, dating from the later sixth and seventh centuries, which is generally thought to represent the burial ground of the Wuffingas and their followers (Figure 9) (Carver 1992; Carver 1998; Newton 1993; Warner 1996, 83–5). King Raedwald himself, first king of the East Angles, may have been buried beneath Mound 1. Less well-known to the general public are the cemetery at Snape, some fifteen kilometres to the north-east, which is slightly earlier in date and which also featured boat burials, together with a wide range of other burial rites; and, only recently excavated, the cemetery at Tranmer House, some 500 metres to the north of the Sutton Hoo site, which dates to the late sixth century (Filmer-Sanky and Pestell 2001; Newman 2000).

The rise of the Wuffingas to power, and their eventual dominance of East

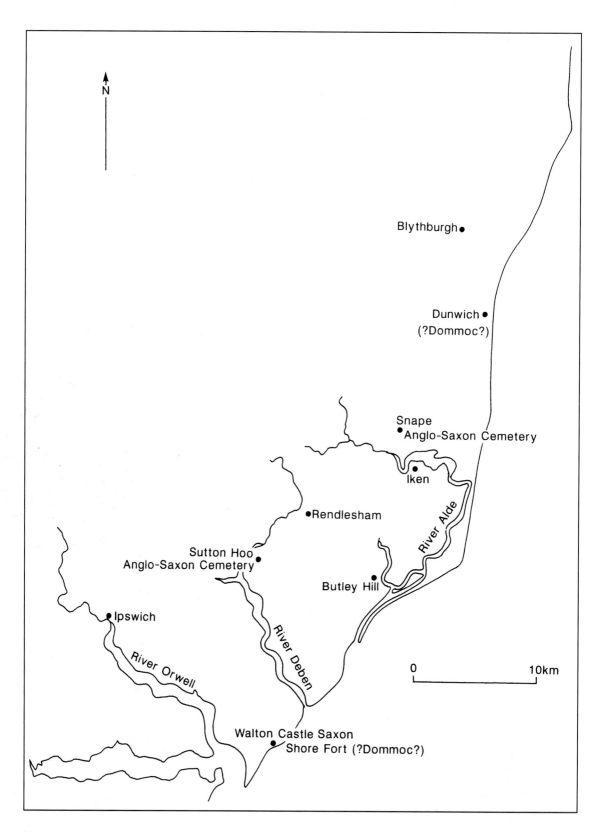

N

Blythburgh●

Dunwich ●
(?Dommoc?)

Snape
●
Anglo-Saxon Cemetery

●
Iken

●Rendlesham

River Alde

Sutton Hoo ●
Anglo-Saxon Cemetery

Butley Hill ●

●Ipswich

River Orwell

River Deben

0   10km

Walton Castle Saxon
● Shore Fort (?Dommoc?)

FIGURE 8.
The principal early and
middle Anglo-Saxon
sites in the Sandlings:
few if any districts in
England can boast such
a concentration.

FIGURE 9.
Aerial view of the great
Anglo-Saxon barrow
cemetery at Sutton
Hoo, perhaps the most
important upstanding
archaeological site in
the Sandlings. The
linear features are
Second World War
anti-glider trenches.

Anglia, is part of a wider phenomenon of the seventh century – the development of recognisable, coherent kingdoms from the fragmented tribal society which emerged from the ruins of Roman Britain. This development was associated not merely with growing social complexity, but with ideological change: with the acceptance, initially by the social elite, of Christianity. Here again the locations of two key sites in the evangelisation of the East Angles reveals the Sandlings as a core area. One was a place called *Dommoc*, possibly the Roman fort at Walton but probably Dunwich, a town which was later the seat of the bishops of East Anglia. Bede, in his *Ecclesiastical History*, describes how Raedwald's son Sigeberht:

> Laboured to bring about the conversion of his whole realm. In this enterprise he was nobly assisted by Bishop Felix, who came to Archbishop Honorious from the Burgundian region, where he had been brought up and ordained, and, by his own desire, was sent by him to preach the word of life to the nation of the Angles ... His episcopal see was established at *Dommoc* (Shirley-Price and Latham 1990, 133).

This was in AD 636. Seventeen years later, following the death of King Anna, the Anglo-Saxon Chronicle records the arrival of another important

missionary: 'Botolph began to build a monastery at *Icanhoh*' (Swanton 1996, 28–9). A number of possible locations for this place have been suggested, including Hadstock in Essex, but the most plausible is Iken, to the west of Aldeburgh. The church here stands on a virtual island, prominently positioned overlooking the estuary of the Alde, a typical site for an early monastery (Figure 10). In 1972 the base of a late ninth-century cross was discovered here, built into the medieval church tower, and subsequent excavations revealed evidence of middle Saxon activity on the site (Cramp 1984; West 1984; Scarfe 1986, 39–51). Not far away – a mere eight kilometres to the south – another middle Saxon site lies on a former island in the marshes, at Burrow Hill in Butley. This, too, was almost certainly a monastery, given its location and the character of the finds made during excavations in the late 1970s (Fenwick 1984), which included imported pottery, window glass, and writing implements. Only seven kilometres to the north-west of Burrow Hill lies yet another important middle Saxon site, Rendlesham, the place where – according to the Anglo-Saxon historian Bede – Swiðhelm, a king of the East Saxons, was baptised by Bishop Cedd. Bede describes it as a *vico regio*, 'royal vill', suggesting that it was one of the main administrative centres in the region. Field-walking has revealed an extensive area of Anglo-Saxon settlement near the church here (Newman 1992, 116–17) although it is possible – as Peter Warner has suggested – that the site of the palace actually lay in what is now the parish of Eyke, which may originally have formed a single territory with Rendlesham (Warner 1996, 116–17). The other major middle Saxon centre in the Sandlings lay some way to the north, at Blythburgh. This maintained its status as an important royal estate into later Saxon times (Warner 1996, 120–1). It was perhaps while defending this place that King Anna and his son were killed at nearby Bulcamp in 654, by a pagan Mercian army led by King Penda. Anna is said to have been buried at Blythburgh and, according to a document called the *Liber Eliensis*, was still being venerated there in the twelfth century (Blake 1962, 18).

The unparalleled collection of early and middle Saxon sites in the southern Sandlings in part reflects the fact that, as we have seen, in the post-Roman period the heavy but fertile clays occupying the centre of the county were largely abandoned, settlement retrenching to the principal areas of light but less fertile soils to either side – i.e., to the Sandlings and Breckland. But in addition, political power in this period rested to a large extent on the control of long-distance trade, and especially trade in prestige goods. Here the Sandling's long and welcoming coastline was of obvious and crucial importance. So too, perhaps, was the fact that this southern part of the district stood, as we have seen, at a crucial cultural frontier: between the south-east of England, with its traditional ties to France and the classical world; and northern East Anglia and north-eastern England, with their contacts with north Germany and Scandinavia. The grave goods associated with the great boat burial at Sutton Hoo certainly suggest close contacts both with Scandinavia, and with Byzantium and Merovingia.

The far-flung contacts of the Wuffingas dynasty are vividly displayed in the rich objects buried at Sutton Hoo. But the main focus of trading wealth was more mundane. From as early as the sixth century, the site of Ipswich seems to have developed as an estuarine *entrepot*, or trading centre, and it grew steadily in size and importance in the course of the seventh and eighth centuries as the main trading place within the East Anglian kingdom and also as a centre for production, presumably under tight royal control. It was here that the distinctive pottery known to archaeologists as Ipswich Ware was manufactured from the early seventh century (Wade 1993).

The Middle Ages

By the time of the Norman Conquest settlement and agriculture had expanded once more on the heavy clay soils of central Suffolk and the Sandlings, like Breckland, had again become a peripheral rather than a core area. It continued to be so throughout the Middle Ages. Todd and Dymond's mapping of the 1327 Lay Subsidy Returns, for example, has shown that 'the light soils of the Breckland in the north-west and the Sandlings in the south-east shared sparser tax-paying populations and raised less tax than the more fertile wood-pasture region of central or High Suffolk' (Todd and Dymond 1999, 80). Nevertheless, the district was not simply an impoverished backwater. Vast flocks of sheep were grazed on the heaths and marshes, and large areas – all but the worst soils – were under cultivation. Above all, the district benefited from the ease of transport offered by the sea and rivers, and by abundant fish stocks, so that significant ports developed at Southwold, Dunwich, Aldeburgh and Orford, the latter a planned settlement associated with a castle erected by Henry II in the 1160s. In addition, markets were established by the thirteenth century at Bawdsey, Kessingland, Sizewell and Covehithe, and by the fourteenth century at Easton Bavents, Blythburgh, and Leiston (Scarfe 1999).

The most important medieval urban settlement in the Sandlings was unquestionably Dunwich. This was already a recognisable town at the time of Domesday, for 'burgesses' are recorded there – 120 in 1066, 236 in 1086, with a further 80 living in the 'suburb' of Alneton in Westleton. There were three churches and the population may already have numbered 3,000. By the thirteenth century there were at least eight parish churches, two friaries, town walls, and two market places (Scarfe 1986, 129–37). However, the settlement was gradually eroded by the sea and, while it maintained some urban functions into the seventeenth century, much of the area of the old medieval town had by this time been lost.

The castle built by Henry II at Orford was not the only one in the district. Another, now completely removed by the sea, existed at Walton, erected by the Bigod family within the ruins of the old Roman fort. Indeed, Orford may have been chosen as a location for Henry's castle in part to limit and control Bigod influence here (their castle was probably destroyed by Henry in 1176). But of more significance in economic and social terms were the various

monastic houses established in the district in the course of the twelfth and thirteenth centuries (Northeast 1999). There were Augustinian houses at Butley and Blythburgh, a Cluniac Priory at Wangford, a house of Premonstratensian Canons at Leiston, and a Benedictine monastery at Snape; the town of Dunwich had two friaries (Franciscan and Dominican), as well as a hospital. In addition, the Cistercian house at Sibton, a little to the west, had extensive holdings in the district. This concentration of religious houses – most of which possessed significant local estates – probably reflects, at least in part, the poor character of the Sandlings soils. When founding or endowing religious houses lay lords tended not to donate more valuable properties, preferring instead to grant away land of relatively low quality, especially if it could be improved significantly under monastic management.

The medieval inhabitants of the Sandlings lived, for the most part, in scattered farms and hamlets, although some larger settlements also existed. They cultivated most of their land in 'open fields', areas of arable in which holdings took the form of small, unhedged, intermingled strips. These fields were most extensive towards the north of the district. To the south, the poor soils ensured that a greater proportion of the land was occupied by heaths. Sheep formed a key element of the economy, valued not only for their meat and wool but also – indeed, mainly – for the dung that they produced. Grazed by day on the heaths or other pastures, and folded by night on the arable land when it lay fallow, they provided a steady stream of nutrients which allowed the easily-leached soils to be kept in cultivation. The great folding flocks were the central, indispensable feature of Sandlings agriculture.

The overall impression is that the Sandlings district in the twelfth, thirteenth and fourteenth centuries had at least moderate levels of population and prosperity. Its medieval inhabitants made the best use they could of the poor sandy soils, and at the same time capitalised on the advantages which nature had given them: the ease of communication and the abundant fish stocks afforded by rivers, estuaries and the sea; and the rich grazing marshes which, as early as the twelfth century, were already being 'inned' from the saltings on some scale.

The post-medieval centuries

In late medieval times the rural hinterlands of the Sandlings may have suffered a measure of decline, for with the drastic fall in population following the Black Death much of England, and especially the more marginal grain-producing areas, experienced a severe agricultural recession. At the same time, other sectors of the economy remained buoyant, and in the Sandlings the principal ports seem to have flourished. The Lay Subsidy of 1524 suggests that Dunwich, Southwold and Walberswick boasted some of the highest densities of taxpayers in the county (Todd and Dymond 1999). In the middle and later decades of the seventeenth century, however, urban prosperity also appears to have declined. The Hearth Tax of 1674 shows not only that most rural parishes carried low populations but also that many of the coastal settlements were impoverished by the decline of herring fishing and boat-building (Evans 1999). This general pattern – of late medieval wealth, followed by comparative early-modern poverty – explains much about the built environment in the Sandlings district, such as the comparative paucity of sixteenth and seventeenth timber-framed buildings compared with the claylands to the west, or the great size of late-medieval churches at places like Blythburgh or Southwold (Figure 43).

But the relative paucity of early timber-framed houses in the Sandlings probably has another cause. The claylands of central Suffolk was mostly fertile land which, from the fifteenth century, developed a thriving cattle-farming and dairying economy. This served to concentrate wealth at the level of the local gentry and yeoman farmers: 'Woodland' Suffolk was a quintessential peasant countryside. The Sandlings was rather different. Here, as in most areas of light, poor soil, the post-medieval period appears to have witnessed the gradual concentration of property in the hands of large estates, and an associated decline in the fortunes, and numbers, of smaller landowners. Light, infertile soils generally encouraged the accumulation of land in large units, together with a steady growth in the size of tenanted farms (Glyde 1856, 383). The poor Sandlings farmers of the sixteenth and seventeenth centuries erected houses which were often too small or flimsy to be maintained by later generations, while in the eighteenth century large estates embarked on the wholesale rebuilding of their farms and cottages. In some cases large estates absorbed the properties not only of small owner-occupiers, but also those of the minor gentry, so that sixteenth-century manor houses like Stutton Hall, Gedgrave Hall or Wantisden Hall had become, by the eighteenth century, tenanted farms. Other uses were sometimes found for gentry residences thus made redundant as their associated estates were absorbed. Following the Dissolution, Butley Priory passed through a number of hands before being acquired by the Wright family, and in 1737 George Wright 'fitted up the gate-house, and by additional buildings and various alterations converted it into a handsome mansion'. By the end of the century, however, the property had been absorbed into the Rendlesham estate and in the 1830s the house was repaired and used 'for the residence of the incumbent' (White 1885, 200).

One of the most important characteristics of the Sandlings was that this gradual concentration of property in the hands of large landowners did not, for the most part, lead to the development of classic 'estate landscapes', with a central core of mansion and park, surrounded by an outer penumbra of estate farms. Indeed, within the area of the Sandlings proper only the Sudbourne estate really fits this classic model. Already, by the early seventeenth century, the Stanhope family owned Sudbourne itself, Iken, Chillesford and much of Orford. A park was laid out around their seat at Sudbourne soon after they acquired it in the 1590s and in 1784 the existing house was replaced by a fashionable brick mansion, designed for the 1st Marquess of Hertford by the architect James Wyatt. The estate's impact on the wider landscape was considerable, for by the later nineteenth century it extended over twenty square miles in a single compact block, 'bounded on three sides by tidal rivers, making it a kind of separate area of Suffolk' (*Country Life* 1901, 240). Most of the other main estates with land on the Sandlings, in contrast, were attached to residences based outside the district in the strict sense, on the claylands to the west. The Tithe Award maps thus show that the Thellusson family owned, by the middle decades of the nineteenth century, the bulk of the parishes of Rendlesham, Wantisden, Capel St Andrew and Butley, together with much of Tunstall, Boyton, Eyke, Sutton, Ramsholt and Alderton (Glyde 1856, 326; IRO P461/153, 202 and 247; FDA 272/A3/1b; FDA 56/A1/1b; FDA 33/A1/1b; FDA 93/A1/1b; FDA 263/C3/1b; FDA 197/A1/1; FDA 3/A1/1b). But their mansion, Rendlesham Hall, was located away from the sands, just outside the western boundary of the AONB. In a similar way, in the north of the region, Benacre Hall formed the core of an estate which embraced Benacre itself, Covehithe, South Cove, and much of Wrentham and Frostendon, as well as farms and properties in some of the neighbouring parishes (IRO FDA 24/A1/1b; FDA 71/A1/1b; FDA 223/1A/1; FDA 302/A1/1b). But once again the mansion of the Gooch family was placed asymmetrically within the estate, on the edge of the clays, although in this case lying within the boundary of the modern AONB. The pattern is repeated a little further to the south where Henham Hall and its park again occupy an area of clay on the fringes of the Sandlings with the estate – owned throughout the post-medieval period by the

Rous family – extending away eastwards into Wangford, Reydon and Southwold. A number of estates based more firmly on the clays also had some holdings on the sands, including Campsea Ashe, which owned part of Tunstall. The reasons for this distinctive pattern will be explored at a later stage: the key point here is that while the Sandlings was, by the eighteenth century, largely owned by substantial landowners, relatively few of them actually lived here. Moreover, in addition to this curious phenomenon of the 'asymmetrical estate', a number of parishes were owned in whole or large part by people whose main properties were located many miles away, patterns of possession which were the consequence of the complex vagaries of purchase, marriage, and inheritance. The Marquis of Bristol, who in the nineteenth century owned much of Bromeswell, thus resided on his estate at Ickworth, near Bury St Edmunds, on the other side of the county. Only in the far south of the modern AONB, on the more mixed soils of the Shotley peninsula, were there a number of more 'normal' estates, on which resident landowners lived in large mansions, with extensive parks, near the centre of their properties, as at Broke Hall in Nacton, Orwell Park, Tattingstone and Woolverston.

Even though great mansions and extensive parks were not a major feature of the Sandlings, in other ways the impact of large estates on the post-medieval landscape was profound. As the holdings of smaller proprietors, copyholders or freeholders, were acquired, the open fields were gradually enclosed, as groups of strips were laid together and surrounded by hedges. In some places, new areas of woodland began to appear, a process which accelerated markedly in the course of the nineteenth century. Above all, the landowners and large tenant farmers of the Sandlings became renowned for their enthusiastic adoption of new husbandry techniques (Wade Martins and Williamson 1999, 106–8). The most important feature of the eighteenth-century 'agricultural revolution' in East Anglia was the cultivation of new fodder crops – roots like turnips, together with clover and other 'artificial grasses' – in regular rotations with cereals. As early as 1674 a note in the manor custumal of Theberton indicates that turnips were already a well-established crop (IRO HA 49/4/14) and a farmer in Tunstall had no less than fifty acres sown with them in 1712 (Burrell 1960, 60). The cultivation of clover also appears to have been widespread by the early eighteenth century. Another key crop came into common use in the course of the eighteenth century, having been grown on a small scale since the early seventeenth: the French tourist Rochefoucauld, visiting in 1784, described 'superb husbandry in very poor soil, and, in particular, the cultivation of carrots for feeding cattle' (Scarfe 1988a, 134).

Clover served to fix atmospheric nitrogen directly in the soil but the main benefit of the new crops was that they allowed higher numbers of sheep and cattle to be kept, and higher volumes of manure to be produced, thus raising cereal yields. In Rochefoucauld's words, 'Through these various methods of cultivation they have a great many cattle and especially sheep, and in consequence a great deal of manure and profit' (Scarfe 1988a, 134). Sheep remained the cornerstone of Sandlings farming: as Arthur Young put it, the poor soils of the district could be successfully cultivated 'only by sheep being made the principal object, and the tillage of the farm absolutely subservient to them' (Young 1795). But the new crops meant that the folding flocks were now managed in a rather different way. The heaths had always provided food for the sheep through both the summer and the winter, the heather shoots providing some sustenance even in the harshest weather. The new root crops now provided additional winter feed and could, moreover, be eaten by the flocks at the same time as they were folded in the fields, thus avoiding the need to walk them each night from heath to arable. The significance of the heaths as 'nutrient reservoirs' was thus reduced and the area under cultivation could, to some degree, be extended at their expense. All in all, according to Rochefoucauld, an 'immense tract of country', comprising 'nothing but shifting sand', had been made very profitable (Scarfe 1988a, 137). Other measures were taken to improve the quality of the poor soils in this period. In particular, in the south of the district coprolites – fossilised dinosaur dung, rich in phosphates – were excavated from the base of the London clay and spread on the fields, a practice which became especially important in the course of the nineteenth century (Armstrong 1973, 2). Until well into the twentieth century, however, sheep remained the supreme source of fertility on these poor, light lands.

Much of the Sandlings landscape evident today was created during this period of agricultural innovation and prosperity in the eighteenth and nineteenth centuries, through the enclosure of open fields and heathland, the reorganisation of existing field patterns by large estates, and the large-scale establishment of woods and plantations to beautify the landscape and provide cover for game. A good deal, however, was created even more recently, in the period after *c.*1900. Developments in this relatively recent period are best understood in terms of two quite distinct chronological phases. From the late 1870s agriculture – in East Anglia as elsewhere – began to slide into a state of recession. Some of the local heaths which had been reclaimed during the agricultural revolution and in the period of Victorian 'high farming' now tumbled back to grass and heather. Moreover, as the recession deepened the heaths were less intensively grazed than before, leading to important changes in their vegetation and ecology. By the 1920s and 30s impoverished landowners were selling large quantities of land to the Forestry Commission, which embarked on a substantial planting campaign on the heaths and derelict arable. The second great phase of change began during the 1939–45 War, and accelerated thereafter. A recovery in farming fortunes, together with changes in agricultural technology, saw a renewed onslaught on the heaths, more dramatic and extensive than anything seen before. Vast areas were converted to arable land, and – from the mid 1950s – the same fate befell much of the ancient grassland of the coastal marshes.

Many of the smaller details of the Sandlings landscape were also created in the period since the late nineteenth century. The holiday industry, although never as important as in some other parts of England, has nevertheless left

FIGURE II.
Beach huts at
Southwold: ephemeral
but distinctive elements
of the modern
landscape of tourism.

a significant mark (Figure II). So too has the Second World War, for the Suffolk coast formed, in effect, England's front line in the war against fascist Germany. Although there are many ancient elements in the Sandlings landscape – Bronze Age burial mounds, great medieval churches, the surviving remnants of the heaths themselves – much of the landscape which we see today was thus created only in relatively recent times.

Representing the Sandlings

The landscape has so far been discussed in this book simply as a reflection, a physical by-product, of past social and economic activities. But the landscape was, and is, also experienced and represented, and the way we think about particular places, and decide which things about them we most value, often derives from how they have been described or illustrated, rather than from how they actually are, or indeed ever were. The Sandlings, however, do not loom as large in the imagined world of art and literature as other distinctive English landscapes. Even if we restrict our attention to Suffolk it is images of Constable's Dedham Vale which spring to mind, rather than representations – visual or literary – of the coast. Although a number of famous writers are associated with the Sandlings, and were doubtless inspired by its scenery – such as George Orwell (whose adopted name was derived from the local river) or Edward Fitzgerald, translator of the *Rubaiyat of Omar Khayyam* – they made little if any direct comment on the landscape. Even Arthur Ransome, who lived for a time at Broke Hall Farm and who describes sailing on the Orwell and along the coast in such books as *We Didn't Mean to Go to Sea*, provides only the briefest of descriptions of the local scenery. George Crabbe, born at Aldeburgh in 1754, was perhaps the first writer to describe the local country-side, in his poems 'The Village' and 'The Borough'. In the former he wrote with enthusiasm about the beauty of the local heaths:

> Stray over the Heath in all its purple bloom
> And pick the Blossom where the wild-bees hum;
> And through the broomy Bound with ease they pass
> And press the sandy sheep-walk's slender grass
> Where dwarfish flowers among the gorse are spread
> And the Lamb browses by the linnet's bed (Edwards 1991, 8)

But few other early writers thought much of the local landscape. Glyde, for example, writing in 1856, described the area between Landguard Point and Dunwich as 'having little to interest the lover of the beautiful in coast scenery' (Glyde 1856, 3). It was only in the later nineteenth and early twentieth centuries, as the growth of the tourist industry led to the expansion of topographic writing and travel literature, that writers began to take a serious interest in the Sandlings. They emphasised the features of the landscape which most modern visitors still find most appealing: the lonely, remote character of the coast and heaths; the melancholy atmosphere; the evidence on all sides for a decline from medieval greatness; the elemental force of the sea; and the traces of remote antiquity in the countryside. Many understandably focused on the site of Dunwich, the great medieval city lost to the sea:

> And so we came to Dunwich, across the wild stretches of gorse-covered heath, weirdly impressive in the strange sunset glow peculiar to flat countries where marshlands abound. Dunwich the desolate, the city of the dead; once the most populous, the most important seaport of these shores ... now a heap of ruins, a handful of crumbling grey stones ... (Berlyn 1898, 199).

The noted topographic writer E. A. Dutt similarly described how 'standing by the weather-beaten church on the cliff', he could

> Scarcely realise that old Dunwich is so completely gone. It seems rather that I must have mistaken my bearings and arrived at some other seabord

hamlet; and that if only I went a little further north or south, I should hear the songs of sailors on the old quays, the voices of merchants in the market place; and see streets thronged with the cosmopolitan crown of a busy port (Dutt 1901, 46)

Such writers were similarly bewitched by the ruins of the great church at Covehithe, symbol both of lost medieval glory and of the insatiable appetite of the sea (Figure 12).

The late nineteenth-century antiquarian M. R. James set several of his famous ghost stories in the district, most notably 'Whistle and I'll Come to You' and 'A Warning to the Curious'. The latter – which concerns the haunting which resulted from the excavation of an Anglo-Saxon barrow – was set at the mythical 'Seaburgh', with its landscape of 'Marshes intersected by dykes to the south ... flat fields to the north, merging into heath; heath, fir woods, and, above all, gorse' (Kneale 1973, 183). Painters, too began to appreciate the beauties of the district in this same period. Some had visited the Suffolk coast even in the early nineteenth century. Peter de Wint and Cornelius Varley, for example, both painted the iconic ruined church of Walberswick (Scott 2002, 18–19). But artistic interest in the area, especially in the countryside around Walberswick, increased during the middle decades of the century and culminated in the 1880s in 'an almost tidal influx' of young painters and etchers into that village, including Phillip Wilson Steer and Edward Stott, many of whom were involved in the New English Art Club, established in 1886 (Scott 2002, 26–49). In the early and middle decades of the twentieth century they were succeeded by a more general migration of literary, artistic and theatrical figures from London. Benjamin Britten came to live in a converted watermill in Snape in 1937 and in 1948 began the Aldeburgh Festival, culminating in the 1960s with the conversion of Snape Maltings into a concert hall.

The artists generally concentrated on the picturesque creeks and the small coastal towns, especially around the Blyth estuary. But many late nineteenth and early twentieth-century writers were equally drawn to the heaths. J. Tennyson, writing in the late 1930s, described how:

A heath, to my mind, is never dull; it is the land of eternal change.
Under the grey skies of winter it is wild and forlorn, exciting and slightly antagonistic; in spring and summer it is a warm, welcoming landscape of ever-deepening colours, brown, yellow, purple and green. And the scents of the heath are scarcely the same for more than two weeks on end ...
(Tennyson 1939, 154).

There is nothing wrong with the romantic, emotive responses to the landscape which we encounter in these kinds of texts. For who can be immune from those feelings of strange melancholy, looking at the waves pounding the soft cliffs at Dunwich? But in this book we will try to look beyond the simple aesthetic appeal of the Sandlings countryside, and attempt to understand the

FIGURE 12.
Covehithe church.
One of the icons of the
Suffolk coast, this vast
half-ruined church
stands only 400 metres
from the soft,
crumbling cliffs.

specific forces and influences – natural and human – which have shaped this unique landscape. Many books on regional landscapes concentrate on how *national* trends and developments are manifested in *local* patterns of settlement and fields or styles of buildings, but my emphasis will be different. The main concern of this book, as may already have become apparent, is to explain the peculiar character of this particular area. To this end we will not attempt to trace the district's development, period by period, century by century, over time. This brief introduction will, I hope, have already provided the reader with this necessary frame of chronological reference. Instead, in the pages that follow we will explore each of the main facets of the landscape – heaths, marshes, fields, settlements and the rest – in turn, giving to each its own place, its own chapter.

CHAPTER TWO

The Coastal Wetlands

....

Fens and marshes

The history of the coastal wetlands is complex, and to understand it we must first define some terms. Early documents tend to refer to three main types of wetland – salt marsh, grazing marsh and fen – and, although these terms were not always very rigorously employed, the three categories were and are at least notionally distinct. *Salt marshes* – the only one of the three to constitute a truly 'natural' environment – developed where the accumulation of silts and marine alluvium, in estuaries or behinds shingle spits or sandbanks, had reached the stage where large areas were only inundated by the highest tides and could be colonised by salt-tolerant vegetation such as sea fern-grass (*Catapodium marinum*) and red fescue (*Festuca rubra*) (Figure 13). Plants like these were of little nutritional value to livestock, and the Suffolk salt marshes do not seem to have been very regularly grazed, at least in historic times. But they did provide a rich store of wildlife which could be trapped and hunted by the local community. The seventeenth-century Suffolk writer Richard Reyce refers to 'those we call seapies, coots, pewits, curlews, teal, wiggeon, brents, duck, mallard, wild goose, heron, crane, and barnacle' caught on the Suffolk coast (Hervey 1902, 35).

Grazing marshes, in contrast, were artificial environments, created by 'inning' areas of salt marsh (Figure 14). Portions were surrounded with embankments – the prominent 'sea walls' which still separate them from rivers or sea – to prevent the ingress of the salt water, and any surface water was allowed to flow away through 'flap sluices', which opened at low tide but were held shut by water pressure when the tide was high. The rich silt or clay-alluvium soils of the reclaimed land made excellent grazing, once the salt had been washed out, and could also be used as arable (Reeves and Williamson 2000). *Fens* were generally less valuable environments. They were found in areas of waterlogged, peaty soils and, while used in part for grazing, they were also cut for a variety of products (Figure 15). Saw-sedge (*Cladium mariscus*) and reed were harvested for thatching; the rough fen grasses and rushes were cut for marsh hay and litter; and some areas were dug for turf or peat, which was used as a household fuel (Taylor 2000).

Most of the areas of reclaimed marsh which existed before the eighteenth century were located in estuaries where the outward flows of rivers and the inward flow of tides had been slowed by the accumulation of sand or shingle spits across the estuary mouths, or in bays similarly sheltered by the development of spits. Fens, in contrast, were either found further inland, higher up the river valleys; or else in estuaries where the accumulation of shingle was so great that the outward flow of watercourses was more seriously impeded, and the regular inward flow of tides prevented. Most fens remained as open common land, exploited by communities living around their margins, until the post-medieval period. Some marshes were also exploited in common: Aldeburgh and Sudbourne, for example, both had 'town marshes', used in a carefully regulated way by the inhabitants (Allen 1982, 77–80, 133–6). Most, however, were private property, even in the Middle Ages.

The distinction between fens and marshes, always blurred, became progressively less clear in the course of the eighteenth and nineteenth centuries, as improvements in drainage technology led to the conversion of many of the former into areas used primarily for grazing. A few fens were reclaimed in the period before 1700 – in 1601 the surveyor John Norden noted, between Rendlesham and Butley, an area of fen beside a brook which had been recently enclosed and turned into good pasture ground (IRO 50/1/74(12)). But on the whole reclamation came late to the peat soils. They were more difficult and more expensive to drain than the salt marshes, and in particular they tended to shrink and compact to a greater extent following drainage. In addition, it was harder to construct embankments of peat than of silt or clay. In 1808, a sea wall was proposed by the Commission of Sewers for the Hundreds of Blything, Mutford, Lothingland and Wangford in order to improve the quality of the marshes along the boundary of the parishes of South Cove, Easton Bavents, and Covehithe. The plan was rejected because:

> The subsoil consists of a loose unconnected horsemuck or weak peat, which would be of little use in raising a wall to bear the pressure of such formidable attacks as it would have to contend with (LRO ST 3361)

Fens and marshes before c. 1750

The reclamation of the coastal marshes began at a very early date, perhaps even in the pre-Conquest period. Extensive reclamations were certainly being made around Orford by the 1160s, following the construction of the great castle there by Henry II. In 1169/70 the Pipe Rolls record payments of £4 11s 7d for 'closing off the Marsh at Orford and ... digging out earth of the same Marsh', presumably a reference to the construction of sea banks to prevent tidal penetration (Allen, Potter and Poulter 2002, 18). There were further payments for 'closing off the Marsh at Orford' in the following year and a neighbouring landowner, one Oslac, was paid compensation for 'his land which was enclosed in the Marsh', suggesting that even the unreclaimed salt marshes might be the property of specific individuals (Allen, Potter and Poulter 2002, 21). The pipe rolls imply that some of the new marshes were on the opposite side of the river Ore to the castle itself, in the area now known as King's Marshes, for in 1170/1 there were not only payments for '700 sheep for the Marsh' but also for purchasing 'one boat for carrying sheep across the waters' (Allen, Potter and Poulter 2002, 21).

Medieval documents make it clear that the grazing marshes were usually divided into discrete properties owned by specific individuals. In the late twelfth century Geoffrey Capra granted Blythburgh Priory a parcel of marsh 'which lies between the marsh which Alexander the son of Walter of Dunwich holds of the canons in Bulcamp and the ... bridge of Bulcamp' (Harper-Bill 1980, no. 70). Parcels of marsh as small as half an acre are described (for example, at Blythburgh: Harper-Bill 1981, no. 486) and various phrases imply a managed, ordered environment. Sometimes the term *fossatum marisci*, 'embanked marsh' is used, and when, in the early thirteenth century, William de Money granted a portion of his marsh in Blythburgh to the Priory he allowed the monks free access to 'the lodge which stands in my marsh' (*logium qui stat in marisco meo*), presumably some kind of isolated marsh farm (Harper-Bill 1980, no. 101).

While much reclamation of the coastal wetlands had thus taken place before the end of the Middle Ages, drainage continued, perhaps at an accelerating rate, into the sixteenth and seventeenth centuries. The salt marshes in Alderton, Bawdsey and Butley were embanked in the 1520s and 30s by Butley Priory. Before this date they had been 'often drowned with salt water and of lyttle valuew' (TNA: PRO E 134 Eliz. 27/28 M15). Henry VIII's sister Mary, her husband the Duke of Suffolk and others went to view the Priory's newly enclosed marshes at Hollesley when they visited the area in 1528 (Dickens 1951, 50), while in the following decade 400 acres (162 hectares) of the Duke of Norfolk's marshes in the same parish were reclaimed, a venture which involved the construction of a sea wall some 370 rods in length. A little later, at the start of the seventeenth century, John Norden's survey of the Stanhope estates shows 'The New Inned Marsh' on the north side of the Butley river, beside the Sudbourne Fleet, as well as the dam erected across the mouth of the fleet to prevent the ingress of the tides (IRO EE5/11/1). In Walton, 247 acres (100 hectares) of saltmarsh were reclaimed in the 1570s; the following decades saw extensive 'inning' in the neighbouring parishes; and walls and a sluice were erected in the 1590s to drain the marshes around Trimley (IRO 50/1/74; TNA: PRO E 134 Car. I M18). In addition to these relatively extensive schemes, there were also innumerable small-scale encroachments onto the salt marshes. A survey of the manor of Walton cum Trimley, made in 1613, thus describes four acres of grazing marsh as 'a new improvement or enclosure latelie inclosed and taken in from the East Cliffe common or the salt marshes' (TNA: PRO E 178 2190).

The process of enclosing and reclaiming the salt marshes was long and complex and can now only be very partially reconstructed. Archaeology can sometimes be used to supplement the evidence of maps and documents. The recent analysis of aerial photographs of the Suffolk coast, carried out by Cain Hegarty and Sarah Newsome as part of English Heritage's National Mapping

FIGURE 13.
View across mudflats
and salt marsh in
Levington Creek. Wild,
natural environments
like this were
progressively 'inned'
and drained in the
course of the medieval
and post-medieval
periods, to create the
rich coastal grazing
marshes.

Programme, has discovered the traces of numerous lost sea walls, rendered redundant (and subsequently levelled) through the further expansion of reclaimed land (Hegarty and Newsome 2005, 81–7). Norden's survey of the Stanhope estates, made in 1600–01 (IRO EE5/11/1), shows that while the marshes in Orford had been embanked and reclaimed by this time, those to the north of the parish boundary in Sudbourne, beside the river Alde, still remained in their natural state – with one exception. The map shows an irregularly-shaped enclosure, 'Thomas Hughes Oxmarsh', lying immediately to the north of the parish boundary (Figure 16). Part of the embankment which surrounded this intake from the saltings remains as an earthwork within the reclaimed marshes. The rest of the circuit, long destroyed, can be picked out on aerial photographs. Evidently, a private landowner in Sudbourne took advantage of the reclamations which had already been made in Orford, using the wall erected along the parish boundary to provide part of the embankment around his 'Oxmarsh'. Some time in the later seventeenth century Sudbourne's marshes were themselves 'inned' by raising a wall against the river Alde; the old banks around the intake were thereby rendered redundant (Hegarty and Newsome 2005, 81–4). More complex stories of reclamation appear on some aerial photographs in the south of Orford parish where, in the words of Hegarty and Newsome, 'a series of relict banks appear to form cells of reclamation, progressing laterally along the course of the river' (Hegarty and Newsome 2005, 85). Only the southernmost and presumably latest bank remains: the others appear only as low earthworks on aerial photographs.

As large, continuous areas of embanked marsh developed, co-operative schemes of flood defence had to be adopted. A Commission of Sewers for the marshes at Orford was established as early as 1561, comprising landowners and tenants who held land on the marsh (Burrell 1960, 123). Like other such bodies, it charged a rent and used the money so raised to maintain and improve the walls and sluices. The body fell into abeyance after a few years, but was replaced in 1601 by another, charged with 'Repayringe amendinge and continuinge of the seawalles beginning in Orford and extending southwardly by the quay and eastwardly by Orford haven to a place called Colting' (Burrell 1960, 123). An area of Sudbourne marshes, known as Haverhill Marshes, was included in its remit. Such Commissions, which continued to be established and re-established well into the nineteenth century, were initially charged only with the maintenance of existing flood defences, rather than with the work of further reclamation. They were, moreover, concerned only with major drainage works – arterial channels and major flood banks – and the upkeep of minor watercourses remained the responsibility of the individual owners and occupiers. Only from the later eighteenth century did they sometimes begin to take a more active role, initiating major improvements in systems of drainage.

Although fens were less valuable than grazing marshes they nevertheless had

FIGURE 14.
A typical view across traditional, unimproved grazing marshes at Shotley. Note the sea 'wall' to the right.

an important role to play in the medieval and early post-medieval economy. *Sandlands*
Fen produce is often referred to in medieval documents. In the middle years
of the thirteenth century, for example, the canons of Blythburgh Priory
reached an agreement with one Hugh de Cressi, in which he conceded to them
the tithes of rushes and turfs (*turbaria*) of all his men in Blythburgh and
Walberswick (Harper-Bill 1980, no. 106). Fens were usually common land and
their enclosure was vigorously opposed by local communities. But some
private fens also existed. In the early thirteenth century, for example,
Blythburgh Priory granted Adam son of Gerard an acre and a rood of turbary
in Sandford which they had been given by Robert son of Ulf, who had himself
bought it from Geoffrey de Marci (Harper-Bill 1981, no. 316). The Priory
received numerous other grants of reedbeds and fens in the twelfth and thirteenth centuries, at Bulcamp and elsewhere (Harper-Bill 1980, no. 98, 111, and
74). Some at least were enclosed by dykes or ditches – in the middle of the
twelfth century the Priory was granted two acres of reed bed (*duas acras
juncherii*) in *Grimesfen* 'enclosed with a ditch' (*fossato inclusas*). There are
numerous references to peat-digging: in *c.* 1200, for example, Geoffrey of
Wenhaston granted three roods of turbary to Sibton Abbey, the document
noting that the monks 'may have all the turf they dig from these three roods
and may dig it out on his land' (Brown 1987, no. 849). As in the Norfolk
Broads, the cuttings seem to have taken the form of long, rectangular pits,
although in this area there is no evidence for the kind of deep excavations
which, once flooded, produced the 'Broads' themselves. In the early thirteenth
century Geoffrey Capra granted two turbaries to the monks of Sibton in
Syremoor in Bulcamp near Blythburgh. One was described as '80 perches and
more long and five wide', with half an acre of 'firm land' beside it; the other
was 80 perches long and six wide, with two roods of firm land. The monks
were to have free access over Geoffrey's land, which they could use to 'dry out,
heap up, and carry away the turves' (Brown 1987, no. 885).

Fens and marshes were often to be found in close proximity. In the early
thirteenth century Geoffrey de Maric granted Blythburgh Priory all his parcel
of marsh in 'Poke*sfen*' (Harper-Bill 1980, no. 77) while a little earlier, around
the middle of the twelfth century, the Priory were granted two acres of reed
bed (*duas acras juncherii*) in *Grimesfen* which lay 'next to the marsh (*marisci*)
of the aforesaid canons which is called *Grantefrith*' (Harper-Bill 1980, no. 101).
Post-medieval maps, likewise, often show fens and marshes lying next to each
other, the former occurring to the landward side of the latter. Nevertheless,
the two broad types of wetland were not distributed evenly and equally along
the coast. The largest areas of fen tended to be in the north of the district –
in the area to the north of Aldeburgh – while the main grazing marshes lay to
the south.

This distribution is, for the most part, a simple consequence of topography.
To the north of Aldeburgh the outfalls of the principal streams and rivers (with
the notable exception of the Blyth) have become completely blocked by banks
of shingle or gravel, seriously impeding their outward flow, preventing regular

ingress of the tide and leading to the creation of swampy lagoons in which peat has formed. Moreover, while extensive areas of silt and clay could also be found in some of these valleys, especially in that of the Hundred River between Benacre and Kessingland, these were harder to drain than the southern wetlands because of the periodic flooding they experienced, either from the ponding back of fresh water behind the shingle spits at time of spate, or from sea water overtopping them during particularly high tides, and then being unable to flow back to the sea. Such areas usually remained only partially improved until the eighteenth or nineteenth centuries. To the south of Aldeburgh the situation was different. The progressive diversion southwards of the river Alde, caused by the growth southwards of Orford Ness, led to the development of extensive areas of salt marsh. The spit restricted, but did not prevent, either the outflow of river water at times of spate, or regular penetration of tidal water. The long, narrow form of these alluvial deposits – forming a band on either side of the river – ensured that areas could be embanked and 'inned' with relative ease, in stages, by constructing 'walls' along the river margins and then back, across a relatively short distance, to the Ness or the mainland. Similar topographic circumstances existed further south, in the area of Hollesley Bay around Bawdsey and Alderton, and along the edges of the Deben and lower Orwell estuaries. In 1664 – when a government Commission reported on the extent of the salt marshes and derelict land on the coasts of Norfolk and Suffolk – the overwhelming majority of the 4,000 acres of unreclaimed wetland it recorded thus lay in the north of the district, with 500 acres noted at Blythburgh, 200 at Reydon, 150 in Wangford and 37 at Walberswick. There were only small quantities noted in the south of the district: in the parish of Sutton, for example, a mere 10 acres remained to be reclaimed (Burrell 1960, 125).

This contrast between the chronology of wetland reclamation in the north and south of the district should not, however, be too sharply drawn. There were areas of early reclaimed marsh in the north, especially in the estuary of the Blyth, where the river mouth was constricted, but never entirely blocked, by a shingle spit, and where the tidal mudflats around Southwold and Walberswick could be 'inned' with little difficulty. Blythburgh Priory received many grants of marsh, as well as of fen, along the estuary during the twelfth and thirteenth centuries, in Bulcamp, Henham and elsewhere, as did Sibton Abbey. Inning and reclamation, often involving the enclosure of former common land, continued here into the sixteenth century. In the 1590s the East Marsh and Pauls Fen in Walberswick were enclosed

> By a wall from an arme of the sea ... and before that time they were not worth above xiid the acre per annum ... the encloseing of them cost one hundred and two of pounds (IRO HA 30/50/22/3.1)

This move was strongly opposed by the commoners, culminating in a murder and a prolonged legal battle which took place during the Civil War (Warner 2000).

In the valley of the Benacre river, similarly, the existence of areas of silt, as well as peat, encouraged some early enclosure and improvement. A map of Benacre, made in 1580, shows a number of islands of enclosed land, described as 'marsh', in the low ground beside the river, surrounded by more extensive tracts of wet common, described as 'fen' – Common Fenne and Holly Fen (LRO PH 629/3/1). Nevertheless, while some attempts at enclosure and improvement had certainly been made, the majority of the wetlands in the north of the district remained unreclaimed, or only marginally improved, at the start of the seventeenth century.

Reclamation of coastal wetlands continued through the seventeenth century – over 200 acres were embanked and drained on the Friston Hall estate in the 1670s and 80s (Burrell 1960, 125) – but thereafter the pace appears to have slowed, probably because most of the most easily inned land had, by this stage, been reclaimed. From the late seventeenth century to the mid eighteenth, population growth was sluggish and farm profits low, and there was thus little money around to invest in expensive schemes of improvement. But as population rose in the second half of the eighteenth century, and especially as prices spiralled upwards during the Napoleonic blockade, landowners began to tackle the remaining, more difficult, areas of wetland.

Wetland reclamation after *c.* 1750

Many of the unreclaimed wetlands in the north of the district, as already noted, were common land, and the late eighteenth century saw a flurry of parliamentary enclosure acts intended to convert them, wholesale, into private property. The commons of Kessingland and Covehithe, including the low wet fens, were enclosed in 1788; those in Uggeshall, Frostenden and South Cove followed in 1799; while those in Sotterley, Henstead-with-Hulverstreet and Wrentham were divided in 1799. The following year Reydon was enclosed and, in 1824, Leiston and Theberton (following a fourteen-year delay – the act itself was passed in 1810) (Tate and Turner 1978). Other more limited areas of wet common seem to have been enclosed by private agreements between principal landowners, without recourse to a parliamentary act. Either way, enclosure was either accompanied, or soon followed, by systematic attempts to improve drainage. One area in which such activities are particularly well documented is the Benacre and Kessingland Level, the low-lying tract to either side of the Hundred River in the extreme north of the AONB. A Commission of Sewers for the Hundreds of Blything, Mutford, Lothingland and Wangford was set up at the start of 1786, and until 1817 was responsible for all the coastal marshes from Aldringham northwards to the county boundary with Norfolk, including those along the south side of the Waveney as far as Bungay (Reinke 1999, 21). Such bodies, as we have seen, levied a rate on local landowners which was used to fund the maintenance of major watercourses, embankments and sluices. In this age of improvement, however, they began to take a more proactive role in drainage matters than they had formerly.

The Commission's earliest minute books show that some attempts had already been made to improve drainage on the Benacre Level (LRO ST 336/1). A 'committee of owners of the level of marshes lying in Benacre' had paid for the construction of a sluice, and this is clearly marked in the sand spit lying across the former estuary of the Hundred River on Hodskinson's map of Suffolk, published in 1783. Much of the land, although poorly drained, comprised silts and clays rather than peat, and was thus potentially good grazing ground and worth such investment. But existing arrangements were, nevertheless, inadequate, and the projected enclosure spurred local landowners

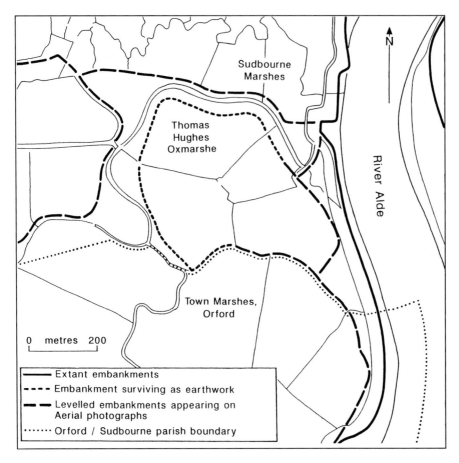

Sudbourne
Marshes

Thomas
Hughes
Oxmarshe

River Alde

N

Town Marshes,
Orford

0   metres   200

—— Extant embankments

---- Embankment surviving as earthwork

— — Levelled embankments appearing on
     Aerial photographs

······ Orford / Sudbourne parish boundary

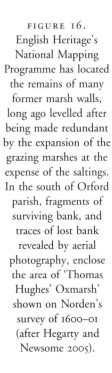

FIGURE 16.
English Heritage's
National Mapping
Programme has located
the remains of many
former marsh walls,
long ago levelled after
being made redundant
by the expansion of the
grazing marshes at the
expense of the saltings.
In the south of Orford
parish, fragments of
surviving bank, and
traces of lost bank
revealed by aerial
photography, enclose
the area of 'Thomas
Hughes' Oxmarsh'
shown on Norden's
survey of 1600–01
(after Hegarty and
Newsome 2005).

into action. The sluice was repeatedly blocked by the further movement of the shingle which had formed the bank in the first place. Moreover, while the bank was enough to impede the outward flow of fresh water, it was frequently overtopped by particularly high tides. As the first entry in the Commission's minute book, for 17 March 1786, put it:

> The level of Marshes [is] … in a very bad state by reason of the water flowing and overflowing from the sea and the stream of fresh water being obstructed in their passage … the sluice lately erected and laid down in this level is not in its present situation [sufficient] to carry water from the said marshes … (LRO ST 336/1)

A new sluice was installed for the Commission by one Nathaniel Lock at a cost of £84, and various other work was carried out in the 1780s in order to improve the flow of water through the Level. New drainage ditches were dug and the river dredged, at a cost of £86. Further work was undertaken in 1793, which included the excavation of a new 'delf' or main drain (LRO 687/1). But problems persisted. The sluice was repeatedly damaged 'by the violence of the sea' and 'the late heavy gales', and – more importantly – it continued to be blocked by the shifting shingle. In 1812 a more comprehensive plan for

improvements was formulated for the Commission by the great civil engineer
and geologist, William Smith. He proposed that a number of existing drains
should be linked together to form two continuous 'landspring dykes', which
would intercept flows of water running off the adjacent upland. These were
to be cut close to 'the boundary between wet and dry land' but were to be
above the level of the former, as 'one of the greatest objects of improving the
drainage [is] that of sending the water down to the Sea on as high a level as
possible'. Smith's plan was evidently to keep the sluice free from shingle by
increasing the velocity of the water flowing through it, and to this end a new
drain was to be laid through the middle of the marsh, in 'as straight as possible
a direction from Latimer Dam to the sluice'. The cost of these projects was
estimated at around £400, with a further £150 for two 'arches' at each end of
the Latimer Dam. This was a considerable amount of money, but Smith was
confident that 'the good effect on the marshes would in the course of next
summer nearly repay the expense'. The Commission accepted the scheme, 'the
Marshes being at present under water'.

Nevertheless, problems with drainage continued, the minute books
recording how the new sluice was either blocked or damaged in 1820, 1821,
1823 and 1827, when – in November – an 'unprecedented high tide ... had
overflown the marshes and filled up the sluice and Delfs leading thereto with
Beach and Shingle'. At this point another famous civil engineer, William
Cubitt, was commissioned to report on the situation and how it might best
be improved. He concluded:

> It appears that the sluice is considerably shorter, both at the Land and the
> Sea ends, than formerly and that the Sea has undoubtedly encroached or
> gained upon the Land during the last 12 or 14 years to the extent of 60 or
> 70 feet, thereby bringing the high water line that much nearer the highest
> point or ridge of the Sand Bank which guards the Marshes ... It appears
> that keeping out the sea altogether in very extraordinary high tides, is not
> so much an object with the Landowners, provided that when it does
> come over, sufficient means could be devised to prevent the drains from
> becoming choked up ... and letting the water off again [but] in my
> judgement the admission of any water over any part of the Embankment
> is decidedly wrong ... because no tide can come over, without in some
> degree washing and lowering the bank (LRO ST 336/1)

Cubitt's preferred solution was to lengthen the sluice, construct a stop-gate
outside it (so that it could be kept dry during repair work) and raise a new
embankment, secured on the seaward side with comprehensive piling. The
proposed cost of £1,500 was too high for the Commission, and neither this
nor a number of alternative plans proposed by Cubitt were adopted. Problems
with drainage on the level, largely caused by the obstruction of the doors of
the sluice by shingle, continued throughout the rest of the nineteenth century,
and constant repairs to both the sluice and associated works were necessary
(Reinke 1999, 30).

The largest area of wetland in the north of the district was the Minsmere Level, covering some 1,600 acres (648 hectares) in the parishes of Middleton, Westleton, Theberton, Dunwich, and Leiston with Sizewell. This low-lying peatland occupied the former estuary of the Minsmere river, finally blocked by a shingle spit some time in the seventeenth century, together with the valley of a minor tributary extending south-eastwards into Leiston. It remained a poorly-drained tract of fen and rough grazing until the establishment, by an Act of 1810, of the Minsmere Level Drainage Trust, composed of all owners of thirty acres or more of land in the Level, or tenants of fifty acres or more (IRO HD 306/2/1; IRO EK 401/1). The Trust's creation followed the passing of the enclosure act for Theberton and Leiston in 1810, although the award itself — formally dividing the commons — did not in fact come until 1824. Moreover, discussions about drainage of the Level, and plans for its improvement, had been mooted by local landowners as early as 1800.

Here, as on the Kessingland Level, the sluice was frequently 'beached up' and the marshes inundated by the sea over-topping the shingle bank. Plans were made for raising the bank and protecting the sluice with piling but action was delayed by a dispute with the engineer, Anthony Bower. Here, too, William Smith was called in to advise. In 1812 and 1813 a new Main Drain was laid out through the middle of the Level, some five kilometres in length. Together with its associated embankments, this cost no less than £1,835. The drain led to a substantial sluice, apparently a more sophisticated structure than that which served the Kessingland and Benacre Level. It was built of iron, and connected to the sea by an iron pipe four feet in diameter, which ran for some 100 metres through the sand and shingle bank. It was cast by Garrett's of Ipswich and completed in 1818. A cottage was built nearby, to provide accommodation for the sluice keeper. Numerous other drains were dug across the common and several existing watercourses stopped or re-directed. Around the same time, a large drain was cut across the middle of Leiston Wet Common, which lay to the south of Minsmere, and this was connected — via another channel, nearly three kilometres in length — to the same sluice (IRO EK 401/1).

Post-medieval drainage schemes, especially in the northern wetlands, sometimes involved the erection of drainage windmills, broadly similar to the more familiar examples on the Norfolk Broads. The earliest were equipped with simple scoop wheels, which lifted the water out of ditches and dykes into a major watercourse linked to the sea. Later, from the nineteenth century, they sometimes drove plunger pumps (Dolman 1978). A drainage mill of some kind was built on the Walberswick Marshes as early as 1743 (Warner 2000, 42) but the surviving examples all appear to post-date *c.* 1800. One has been re-erected and restored at the Museum of East Anglian Life at Stowmarket by the Suffolk Mills Group: it is a small wooden smock mill equipped with fantail and the self-regulating 'patent' sails, rather like Venetian blinds, which had been invented by William Cubitt at the start of the century. Those that remain *in situ* are less well preserved. The small tower mill at Chillesford Lodge, Gedgrave (TM 468583) was built in the early nineteenth century, raised in height later in the century, restored in the 1950s but then tailwinded in a storm and largely destroyed, so that only the lower storey, with the remains of the scoopwheel, survives. Similarly scant traces remain of a second mid nineteenth-century smock mill erected on the Minsmere Level (TM 475659); while at Aldeburgh (TM 468583) only the foundations exist of a smock mill built around 1800. At Leiston the Sea Wall Mill, again of early nineteenth-century date, was badly damaged by gunning practice during the 1939–45 War and collapsed completely in 1976 (Dolman 1978, 51). More survives in the case of Blackstone Mill at Reydon (TM 491759) and Walberswick Marsh Mill (TM 486736), for these were brick towers, like the majority of the drainage mills on the Norfolk Broads; both, however, are now only empty shells. That at Walberswick, in particular, is a picturesque feature of the landscape, now standing somewhat incongruously in the midst of extensive reed beds (Figure 17). Drainage windmills were never as common on the coastal wetlands as they were on the Broads, but the Ordnance Survey First Edition six inch maps of the late nineteenth century show a number of additional examples, which have now completely disappeared. Three 'windpumps' are thus marked within the Lantern Marshes, in the lee of Orford Ness; these, and some other examples, were perhaps no more than simple trestle or skeleton mills, rather

FIGURE 17.
A drainage windmill was erected on the Westwood Marshes, to the south of Walberswick, as early as 1743, but the surviving structure here is of early nineteenth-century date.

than the kinds of larger structures just described (which the nineteenth-century Ordnance Survey maps usually dignify with the term 'windmill pump').

Not all schemes of improvement in the period after 1750 were, like those on the Minsmere or Kessingland Levels, carried out by corporate bodies. There were also many private initiatives, like those made by the Rous estate on the northern side of the Blyth estuary, in Bulcamp, Henham and Reydon. A map of 1765 shows some 273 acres of unreclaimed marsh lying between the Blyth and the Southwold-Blythburgh road. By 1800, the whole area had been enclosed and 'inned', a new pattern of drainage dykes laid out, and the course of the river itself straightened (Burrell 1960, 143). Moreover, as farming incomes soared in the years around 1800, improvements were also made to the drainage of some areas of silt marsh which had been reclaimed centuries before. A Commission of Sewers for Felixstowe and Falkenham, for example, was set up in the 1780s to simplify and improve the drainage on 945 acres of marsh held by 19 different owners (Burrell 1960, 140–1). New drainage commissions were established for Orford and Sudbourne, and for Iken, in 1852 (IRO HA3:50/10/2.2), although the former only appears to have met from 1868 and the latter from 1871. Their minute books detail the money expended on the maintenance of flood banks, sluices and some dykes, and show that expenditure fluctuated significantly, partly in response to natural conditions, such as the damage caused by particularly high tides (like that of 1877) (IRO HA5:50/102.1; HA5:50/10/2.2). In the case of the Iken Level, annual expenditure rose gradually from £51 in 1871 to £270 in 1879. The rates levied mirror this, climbing from 1s 6d per pound value of property to 10 shillings in 1879. Both then fell back again, averaging £100 and 3 shillings respectively through the later 1880s and 1890s, perhaps reflecting the declining fortunes of local farmers as the agricultural recession began to bite.

In terms of landscape character, the differences between the coastal marshes reclaimed before 1700, and areas only drained in the eighteenth and nineteenth centuries, are still apparent. Wetlands of the latter type usually have a highly rectilinear pattern of dykes: the former, in contrast, usually include a high proportion of irregular or serpentine channels, adapted from the natural pattern of salt marsh drainage when the areas in question were first 'inned'. The distinction is not absolute, it is true, and the line between the two categories is sometimes hard to draw, in part because the silt marshes are seldom *entirely* drained by serpentine and irregular dykes. Most also feature some straight drains, evidently added at a subsequent date in order to improve drainage. Thus John Norden's survey of the Stanhope estates, made in 1601, shows a relatively sparse pattern of irregular dykes on the Lantern marshes behind Orford Ness (IRO EE5/11/1). By the 1880s, when the Ordnance Survey First Edition six inch maps were surveyed, these had been supplemented by a much denser pattern of ruler-straight ditches, at some of the major intersections of which small drainage windmills had been erected. Like all landscapes, that of the coastal marshes was always changing. Nevertheless, the essential distinction between areas with a high proportion of serpentine dykes and areas

FIGURE 18.
The Sandlings, showing the distribution of the different types of coastal wetland.

dominated by rectilinear patterns is still evident in the landscape and – not surprisingly, given the previous discussion – the former tend to dominate the wetlands to the south of Aldeburgh, and the latter those to the north (Figure 18).

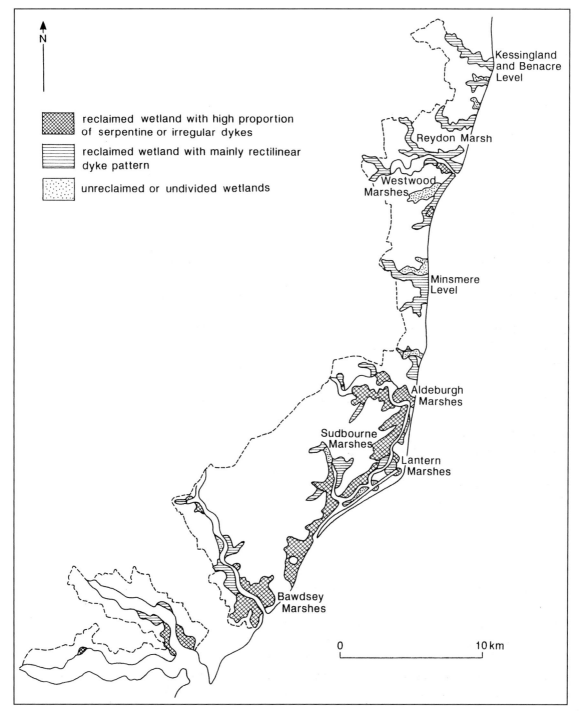

The wetland economy

The coastal wetlands, even in their unreclaimed state, offered a number of important resources to the local inhabitants, especially in the form of fish and shellfish. But the exploitation of such things has left few obvious traces in the landscape. The remains of a fish trap of probable middle Saxon date has recently been discovered in Holbrook Bay. It is composed of two rows of paired posts (once probably supporting a wattle fence) which meet at a point, forming a 'V' (Hegarty and Newsome 2005, 61–3). Others, of the type known as 'kiddles' and originally featuring nets rather than fencing, are known from the inter-tidal zone off Stonner Point in the Deben estuary, and are probably of medieval date (Hegarty and Newsome 2005, 105). More ubiquitous and obvious, however, are groups of rectangular or sub-rectangular oyster pits found in the estuarine inter-tidal zone just beyond the river wall, especially in the lower reaches of the river Ore, and along the Butley river. Oysters occurred naturally on the floors of the local creeks and estuaries and were caught by dredging from an early date; Norden's survey of the Stanhope estates (1600–01) shows two 'oyster boates' at work in the Butley river (IRO EE5/11/). The right to take these and other shellfish belonged to manorial lords and were leased to particular individuals, although there were frequent disputes: in 1751 three fishermen were thus prosecuted for taking 1,000 bushels of oysters from Shottisham Creek, where one Thomas World claimed exclusive fishing rights (IRO HD 1409/1); and in the seventeenth and eighteenth centuries the men of Aldeburgh and Orford frequently disputed the right to take oysters from the Alde (Allen 1982, 70). In addition to harvesting purely natural communities, however, oyster beds could also be deliberately 'seeded' using stock from pits specially dug for the purpose, a practice which probably began in the area only in the nineteenth century (HA93/8/39–50). The individual pits can range from around two metres square to as much as 70 metres in length, and can form groups numbering anything up to thirty. Several examples were still in use when the Ordnance Survey First Edition six inch maps were made in the 1880s.

Salt production was another important coastal activity, and the sites of 28 'red hills' – irregular mounds of salt-production debris of Roman date – are now known from the Suffolk coast, preserved (or preserved until recently) within areas of reclaimed grazing marsh (Hegarty and Newsome 2005, 55–9). Most are in the south of the district, where the areas of salt marsh have always been most extensive. Salt production continued into medieval times – Domesday records a number of salt pans along the coast (and also in a number of inland vills, presumably detached assets of the manors in question) and one was constructed as part of Henry II's development of the town of Orford in the 1160s (Darby 1957, 187–8; Allen, Potter and Poulter 2002, 22). Coastal salt production declined in importance, here as elsewhere in England, during the post-medieval period but did not disappear entirely. The Southwold salt works was at its peak in 1750, largely supplying the local fisheries, and its warehouse at Blackshore Wharf was capable of holding more than a thousand tons of salt. It finally closed in 1900 (Williamson 1996).

Following their enclosure and reclamation, agriculture – and in particular livestock production – was by far the most important activity on the marshes. In the early medieval period sheep were the principal stock grazed on most coastal marshes in England but by the late Middle Ages their place was usually taken by cattle. The Suffolk marshes followed this national trend to some extent, for by the sixteenth century dairying and bullock fattening were a major part of the local economy, but sheep continued to be of some importance. Many of the bullocks were northern 'stores' from Scotland or Ireland, brought in by drovers (Burrell 1960). The stocking densities on the best marshes were extraordinarily high. On the Friston estate it was anticipated in 1692 that no fewer than fifty head of cattle could be fattened in the summer, and 300 wether sheep in the winter, on 100 acres (40 hectares) of reclaimed marsh (Burrell 1960, 145). But the quality of the grazing clearly varied from place to place. A survey of the Rathbone estates made in 1613, for example, shows that some of the marshes were rented at between ten and twelve shillings an acre per annum, but others for as little as two shillings (IRO 50/1/74).

The stock were grazed on the marshes for much of the year – the herbage was particularly valuable for the folding flocks in the spring – but they were generally taken off them in the winter, partly to prevent 'poaching' of the wet ground but also because the grass growth was meagre during the winter months. The sheep would be moved to upland heaths or onto root crops in the arable fields, while the cattle were often 'yarded' and fed on hay or turnips. Traditional management of the marshes involved keeping the water level in the dykes relatively high during the summer, for they not only drained the land but also served as 'watery fences' which defined different properties and prevented livestock from straying from one area of marsh to another. This is why hedges and fences were rarely found on grazing marshes – the dykes fulfilled their functions – although they are sporadically referred to in documents (an agreement to divide land in Tinkers Marsh, Walberswick, drawn up in 1766, thus refers to the erection of a 'sufficient hedge, ditch and fence': HA30:50/22/3.48). In most cases, the dykes also provided drinking water for livestock, although towards the sea wall the water was often fairly brackish. Indeed, it was (and is) the transition from brackish to fresh water within the marsh dykes which provides much of the environmental interest in traditional grazing marshes, although their real importance in this respect derives from the fact that they provide a habitat for large breeding populations of waders and wildfowl, attracted in part by the character of the grass sward maintained by cattle grazing, and in part by the fact that the maintenance of a high water table ensures that worms and other invertebrates are concentrated in the upper levels of the soil, and are thus easily accessed by the birds (Beardall and Casey 1995, 54–5).

The Suffolk coastal marshes were always used mainly for grazing but, like those found elsewhere in England, they might on occasions be cultivated, for arable crops. As John Kirby noted in 1735, the marshes 'sometimes, when ploughed, afford the greatest crops of corn of any other land in this country' (Kirby 1735, 2). Numerous seventeenth- and eighteenth-century maps show areas called 'ploughed marsh', 'rye marsh', or 'wheat marsh'. Examples include a survey of Dodnish Manor Farm in Falkenham, made in 1766 (IRO 79/2/2); a map of Iken Hall estate, dating to 1841 (IRO HD 628/4); a map of 1731 showing the Ipswich Corporation lands in Kirton (IRO C3/8/1/13); and a 1733 survey of the Leathes estate in Walton, which features both a 'Hither Ploughed Marsh' and a 'Further Ploughed Marsh' (IRO HA 403: T 1039/13) (Figure 19). Many landlords used prescriptive leases to prohibit or at least limit the extent of cultivation – one for Aldeburgh Hall, drawn up in 1712, stated that no marshland was to be ploughed beyond that already in cultivation (IRO 331 Box 17). But the pressure to convert the marshes to arable increased in the late eighteenth century, especially as grain prices rose to unprecedented heights during the Napoleonic blockade. One farm in Butley had 38 out of 104 acres of its marshes under the plough in 1794 (Burrell 1960, 147); another in Alderton, in 1813, was cultivating 34 out of 92 acres (IRO 427/905). When prices fell back after the end of the War, however, arable use declined again and by the time the Tithe Award maps were surveyed in the years around 1840 few of the marshes were in tilth.

Fens, as already noted, were used in different ways to marshes. They were primarily cut, rather than grazed, and never ploughed. The names used on

FIGURE 19.
Extract from a map of the Cartaret Leathes estate in Walton, surveyed in 1733: note the areas named 'Ploughed Marsh'.

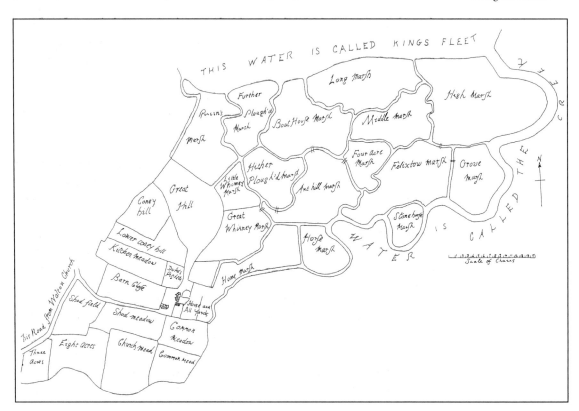

44

early maps sometimes refer to their use or condition: 'Rushy Fen', 'Mowing Fen' and 'Horse Fen' are particularly common, the latter reflecting the fact that, when subject to grazing after they had been mown, horses were considered particularly appropriate consumers of their coarse vegetation. The improvements in drainage carried out in the course of the eighteenth and nineteenth centuries drastically reduced traditional forms of exploitation. Although some areas remained only minimally drained (like The Fens in Aldringham-cum-Thorpe) the old forms of management gradually declined. Reed beds ceased to be systematically exploited, and peat cutting had largely died out by the end of the nineteenth century, even the poor now usually burning coal in their grates.

One particular feature of the economy of the Sandlings wetlands deserves a brief mention. Decoys were a method of trapping wildfowl introduced from Holland in the early seventeenth century (Payne Gallwey 1886; Wentworth Day 1981). They consisted of a number of curving 'pipes' – tapering channels covered by netting, supported on a framework of hoops of wood or iron – leading off from an area of open water. Each pipe terminated in a long bow-net which could be detached from the rest of the apparatus. Along one side of each pipe was a series of overlapping screens, usually made of wood and reeds, behind which the decoy man would conceal himself. Wildfowl were lured into the net by using a combination of tame decoy ducks and a dog called a 'piper'. The former were trained to enter the pipe when commanded to do so by a low whistle from the decoy man; at the same time the dog would run around the screens, jumping over the low boards or 'dog jumps' placed between them. The wild fowl gathered near the mouth of the pipe were attracted towards what – to them – must have looked like an appearing and disappearing dog. Encouraged by the behaviour of the decoy ducks, they swam towards it. When they had proceeded some way the decoy man would appear, waving his arms or a handkerchief and driving the birds in flight down the tapering pipe, and into the bow net.

The earliest known decoy in England was at Waxham on the north-east coast of Norfolk where, as early as 1620, Sir William Wodehouse had constructed 'a device for catching DUCKS, known by the foreign name of a koye' (Payne Gallwey 1886, 2). That at Purdis Farm, to the east of Ipswich and a few kilometres outside the AONB, must have been almost as old, for it is mentioned in a lease of 1646 (HA 93/3/48). It is the best documented decoy in Suffolk, appearing regularly in estate documents drawn up over the following 270 years. A particularly detailed description is included in a survey of 1862 (IRO HA 93/3/163). By this date there were two ponds: the larger 'Duck Pond' had six pipes (a development from the situation in 1813, when an estate map recorded three: HA 93/12/39) and the smaller 'Teal Pond' had two. The site was said to be worth £181 2s 0d *per annum*. A number of other decoys were established in the district in the course of the seventeenth and early eighteenth centuries. That at Chillesford was constructed before 1736 (it is depicted on Kirby's county map of that date) and continued to operate until at least the mid-1880s (Payne Gallwey 1886, 163; IRO HD11 475/867; HD 475/870). Those at Iken and Friston also appear on Kirby's survey: the former, which was sometimes leased with the adjacent warren, was still working in the 1920s, but the latter had ceased to operate by *c.* 1830 (Payne Gallwey 1886, 163–8; IRO FC 161/N1/4; Whittaker 1918, 76) (Figure 20). Other examples were constructed in the nineteenth century, more as gentleman's hobbies than commercial concerns: that at Nacton, for Sir Robert Harland, in 1835; that at Benacre, for Sir Francis Gooch, in *c.* 1880 (Payne Gallwey 1886, 166). There were other decoys a little further back from the coast, at Campsea Ashe, Marlesford, and Melton. Vast numbers of wildfowl were taken. At Iken, for example, no fewer than 2,846 were trapped in the year 1879–80 (Payne Gallwey 1886, 163), while at Nacton 9,303 were taken in 1925–26 (Matthews 1969).

Decoys were prominent features of the local landscape, and are singled out for particular representation on the various early maps of the county. As in other parts of England, however, their numbers declined steadily during the second half of the nineteenth century, in part because of changes in dietary habits, in part because improvements in drainage reduced the numbers of wildfowl in the environment, and in part because of competition from recreational shooting. The decoy at Iken, as we have seen, continued to function into the 1920s, but ceased soon after: that at Nacton was operated sporadically into the 1960s and was then taken over by the Wildfowl Trust.

FIGURE 20.
Survey of a farm in Iken, 1841, showing reclaimed heathland to the west (left), grazing marshes to the east (right), and duck decoy.

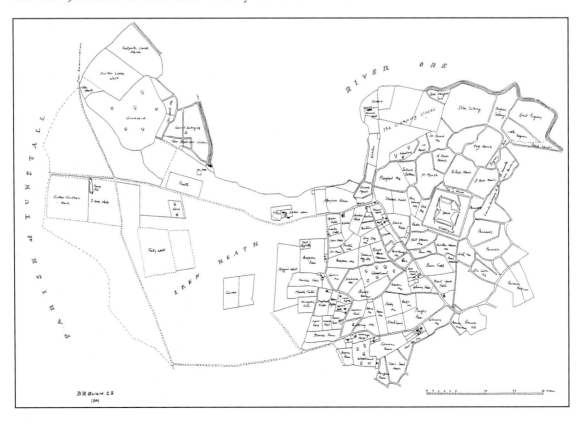

FIGURE 21.
A number of wetland areas, reclaimed and improved in the nineteenth century, reverted to fen and reedbed in the course of the twentieth century, as here at Friston, on the north shore of the Alde estuary.

The recent history of the fens and marshes

The great agricultural recession which began in the late nineteenth century, and which continued with little intermission until the outbreak of the Second World War in 1939, led to the neglect of drainage and the reversion of some areas of reclaimed wetland to reed beds. Notable examples include the Westwood Marshes in Blythburgh and Walberswick, which were progressively abandoned in the course of the twentieth century and which today constitute one of the largest and most environmentally important areas of reedbed in eastern England; and various areas around the margins of Butley Creek and the Alde and Blyth estuaries, where extensive reedbeds developed within walls which were breached and never subsequently repaired (Figure 21). The deterioration in drainage conditions was in general less marked on the old-enclosed silt marshes than on the reclaimed peat fens, for this was more valuable land and worth preserving from the sea even in a period of poor agricultural prices. But with the return of agricultural prosperity in the second half of the twentieth century the landscape of the marshes changed dramatically. The drive to increase production, which continued under successive post-War governments

47

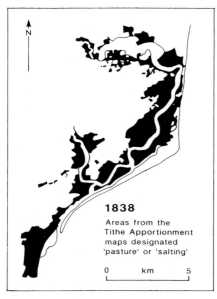

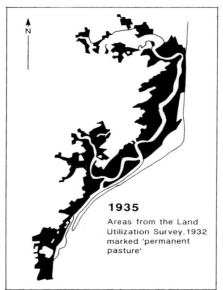

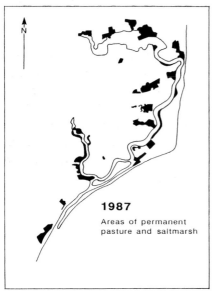

FIGURE 22.
The contraction of
coastal marsh in the
Alde/Ore estuary, 1838
– 1987 (after Beardall
and Casey 1995).

and especially following Britain's entry into the European Economic
Community, led to their wholesale conversion to arable.

Between 1948 and 1953 100 acres (40 hectares) of marsh were ploughed in
Felixstowe, just outside the area of the AONB (Trist 1971, 129); in 1952
J. W. Mann broke up 155 acres (63 hectares) on Ferry Farm, Sudbourne; and
in the years following the end of the War various small areas were ploughed
elsewhere. But it was the disastrous floods of 1953 which, in Trist's words,
marked 'the turning point in the history of production on the Suffolk
marshes' (Trist 1971, 130). The sea walls were raised by *c.* 0.6 metre to
provide protection against further incursions from the sea, and pumps were

widely installed to replace gravity sluices. After the flood much of the marsh lay in an unproductive, saline state for two years, but with drainage conditions significantly improved, and with important changes in the relative value of livestock as opposed to arable produce, the conversion to arable began in earnest. Between 1955 and 1958 every marsh ditch on the 20,000 flooded acres was excavated and 5,000 acres were ploughed. The new pumps allowed a lower water level to be maintained in the dykes and this in turn made it possible to install under drains, three-inch clay pipes laid, in most cases, at intervals of *c.* 30 metres, in order to drain the whole of the land more effectively (Trist 1971, 130–2). In most places the existing pattern of curvilinear dykes was maintained but some new watercourses were installed and at The Firs in Sudbourne an entirely new rectilinear dyke pattern was created. Drainage improvements, along with arable conversion, continued apace and by 1970 another 3,500 acres had been ploughed. Today, the overwhelming majority of the silt marshes are under arable cultivation, and most of the rest now comprises improved, chemically farmed grassland. Only a few areas have continued to be managed in the traditional way, with a high water table, most notably Sizewell Belts and Tinkers Marsh at Walberswick, although some of the improved marshes have, over recent decades, begun to be managed once again in the traditional way by conservation bodies, including Hazelwood and Church Farm Marshes. Nevertheless, the total area of unimproved coastal and estuarine grazing probably amounts to less than 300 hectares, out of a total wetland area of 10,000 hectares (Figure 22) (Beardall and Casey 1995, 52–4). The twentieth-century destruction of the coastal marshes has been a great tragedy, in both environmental and historical terms, and every encouragement should be given to those actively preserving this small and precious remnant, and attempting to return more areas of improved marsh to their traditional state.

CHAPTER THREE

The Heaths

....

Introduction

Heaths remain perhaps the most distinctive element of the Sandlings landscape, although their area has contracted considerably since the start of the twentieth century, large areas having been converted to arable, built on, or planted up as conifer plantations. All English heaths, in spite of their untouched, 'natural' appearance, were created by man, for all were originally tree-covered. But they lie on sandy soils which, because they are easy to cultivate, were attractive to early farmers. Once cleared of trees, their soils deteriorated, leading in time to the development of the characteristic soil of the heathlands, the *podzol*, in which grey upper levels, leached of humus and iron, overlie hard layers of 'pan' where these have been redeposited (Rackham 1986, 286–91; Dimbleby 1962). Once they ceased to be cultivated, the poor acid character of these soils, coupled with constant grazing by sheep and other livestock, favoured the development of a characteristic vegetation, dominated by various combinations of heather or ling (*Calluna vulgaris*), bell heather (*Erica cinerea*), gorse or furze (*Ulex europaeus*) and broom (*Sarothamnus scoparius*). Characteristic grasses also thrive in such an environment, including sheep's fescue (*Festuca ovina*), wavy hair grass (*Deschampsia flexuosa*), and common bent (*Agrostis tenuis*), while some areas become dominated by bracken.

Not all English heaths are the same. Those in the Sandlings fall, for the most part, into the type classified in the National Vegetation Classification scheme (the standard system used by ecologists to categorise British plant communities) as *H1 – Calluna vulgaris – Festuca ovina* heath. This is a type which is found across much of East Anglia, especially in the Breckland of north-western Suffolk and south-western Norfolk (Rodwell 1991, 372–8). It is the most continental of the British heaths, 'an impoverished relative of the *Genisto-Callunion* heaths of north Germany and the Low Countries' (Rodwell 1991, 372). Its main characteristic is the relatively limited number of species present. Ling (*Calluna vulgaris*) is the only, or overwhelmingly dominant shrub, bell heather and gorse being largely excluded by climatic factors – rainfall is too low, and the annual temperature range too great, for them to thrive (Figure 23). However, these species do occur in some numbers on the Sandlings heaths, although usually only as relatively limited stands, probably

because the proximity of the sea serves to ameliorate these climatic factors. Such is the dominance of heather that even the grass *Festuca ovina* is often present only as scattered tussocks: other grasses, such as *Agrostis cappilaris*, are even more confined (Rodwell 1991, 374–5).

Although the classic heather-dominated heaths are the most striking of the semi-natural landscapes of the sandy uplands, in some places grass heath – acid grassland dominated by common bent, sheep's fescue, and sheep's sorrel (*Rumex acetosella*) – occurs (Beardall and Casey 1995, 32–3). The distribution of grass heath is imperfectly understood but may be a function of historical as well as ecological processes. Some areas of the Sandlings heaths have been ploughed in the past, and it is possible that some at least of the grass heaths represent areas which were under cultivation for such extended periods that heather has had difficulty in re-establishing itself. For the most part, however, the grass heaths seem to correspond with soils formed, in part, in the more calcareous crag deposits, rather than solely in the glacial sands which dominate most of the higher ground in the district.

Heaths do not constitute a stable 'climax' vegetation. They were not only created, but are also sustained, by human activities. When the intensity of grazing on heaths is reduced or curtailed – as happened throughout southern England in the course of the twentieth century – the character of the vegetation changes rapidly. Although large areas of open heather still survive on the Sandlings, as at Dunwich or Sutton, the reduction in the intensity, or the complete cessation, of grazing means that many have degenerated into rather rougher land. On Westleton Heath, for example, while much open heather remains, large areas are being invaded by bracken and by a scatter of hawthorn, sloe and birch. Here active management holds the situation in check but elsewhere, as on Snape Warren or Blaxhall Heath, degeneration to scrub and woodland proceeds apace (Figure 24). It is difficult for hawthorn, birch or oak to successfully colonise dense stands of heather. But the older, more degenerate stands which develop once the intensity of grazing declines provide more open ground. Once the trees become established they shade out the heather, leading eventually to the development of the *Quercus-Betula-Deschampsia* woodland which is the natural climax vegetation on these poor soils (Rodwell 1991, 377).

Not only the cessation of grazing, but also the demise of other traditional management practices, has taken its toll. In the past, bracken was regularly cut from the heaths for use as thatch and animal bedding, and the grazing stock would trample and eat the young regenerating fronds, thus holding it in check. On most heaths neither of these things now happens. Most, moreover, are dominated by even-aged, rather old stands of heather. Regular cutting and grazing formerly ensured both regular regeneration and a more varied age structure but now as the old plants die back the areas they occupied are easily invaded by the vigorous growth occurring on the edge of bracken areas. For all these reasons, bracken is a far more prominent component of the heathland vegetation than formerly, often dominating extensive areas to the exclusion of other plants (Figure 25). In addition to all this, ungrazed heather develops dry woody layers which can pose a serious fire risk in dry weather. Heaths, in short, have become a threatened resource in the course of the twentieth century. Fortunately, their value has recently come to be more widely appreciated, and considerable steps have been taken over the last few years to arrest the decline of those in the Sandlings.

The origins of the heaths

In many parts of England heaths were first formed in remote prehistoric times and continued as open, treeless ground right up until the present (Dimbleby 1962). But this was not always the case, and some areas now occupied by heathland appear to have been woodland or wood-pasture in the Middle Ages, either because they had never been fully cleared, or because woodland reclaimed them in the immediate post-Roman period, when the population fell dramatically and land was used less intensively. The Sandlings heaths were probably largely cleared by late prehistoric times but a surprising number of major place names in the southern Sandlings suggest the presence of Saxon woodland – Shotley, Trimley, Hollesley, Hemley, Ramsholt, Waldringfield, Butley, Gedgrave, and Hazelwood all incorporate Anglo-Saxon terms for woods, or for clearings within woodland (*leah, holt, feld, wudu*). Charcoal remains recovered from the enigmatic 'burnt stone features' excavated at the Anglo-Saxon burial ground at Snape included examples of both Scots pine and oak (Filmer-Sankey and Pestell 2001, 223–6). The pines at least had probably grown in the immediate vicinity. Some areas now occupied by heathland may thus, in Saxon times, have resembled the densely-timbered wood-pasture at Staverton (below, pp. 105–8). Domesday Book records very little woodland in the district, except towards the north, where some vills extended up onto the claylands to the west: Aldringham, for example, had woodland sufficient for 500 swine. To the south, Staverton had sufficient for thirty, but elsewhere only negligible quantities were recorded. Sudbourne, for example, had woodland for only twelve pigs, perhaps equivalent to twenty acres or so; and at Snape there was woodland sufficient for a mere six swine.

Most of the woodland apparently indicated by local place names presumably degenerated in the course of the later Saxon period through over-grazing, as population rose again and pressure on land intensified. Westwood in Blythburgh may not long have lost its tree cover when, some time before 1230, the Priory received a grant of twelve acres of heathland there (Harper-Bill 1980, no. 43). But some woodland may have been deliberately assarted – that is, cleared to make way for arable land. A number of field names recorded in medieval documents appear to refer to woodland clearance, like the half acre called *Redynges* in Blythburgh, granted to the Priory in the early thirteenth century (from the Old English *hryding*, 'a clearing') (Harper-Bill 1980, no. 38). Early charters occasionally refer directly to newly-cleared ground, like the 'three acres of assarts (*de essarto*) in Westgate' which the Blythburgh monks received in the early thirteenth century, although the term assart was used to describe intakes from heathland, as well as clearances of woodland.

In some parts of England the overwhelming majority of heaths were common land, but in the Sandlings this was not the case: large areas were held as private property. Numerous grants of heathland are thus mentioned in the early charters of the area, like the 'heath called *Hulsatum*' in Blythburgh, granted to the Priory there in the mid twelfth century (Harper-Bill 1980, no. 42). At the end of the century Robert son of Reginald of Dunwich granted the Priory 'all the heath which he holds in Blythburgh, which the canons shall hold after his death for an annual rent of 12d' (Harper-Bill 1980, no. 45); while the monks of Sibton were given two parcels of heath in Westleton in *c.* 1240, one on 'Stonhil', the other on 'Kaluehil' (Brown 1986, no. 83). Ecclesiastical

FIGURE 24.
Silver birch trees
regenerating over
ungrazed heathland on
Hazelwood Common.

houses alienated, as well as received, areas of heath: in the early thirteenth
century Blythburgh granted William of Dunwich 'all our heath in the vills of
Henham or Wangford called *Grethal*' (Harper-Bill 1980, no. 319).

Much heathland was thus already demesne land in medieval times – part of
the 'home farms' of medieval lords. But the extent of private heath evidently
increased in post-medieval times, as major landowners succeeded in enclosing
portions into private 'walks'. In 1526 the men of Orford rioted, 'breaking down
hedges and filling in ditches' which had been created by Butley Priory at
Gedgrave, and claiming to have rights of common over the land in question
(Dickens 1951, 50). Norden's survey of the Stanhope estates, made in 1600–01,
shows a number of examples of recent enclosure and appropriation (IRO
V5/22/1; EE5/11/1). In the south-east of Bromeswell, for example, one area of
sheepwalk is separated from the adjoining common heath by 'the ditch of the
new Inclosure', while in Eyke a large tract of heathland is simply described as
'Late Common'. Moreover, by this time many manorial tenants also held
their own individual portions of heath. A map of Sutton, surveyed in 1631, for
example, shows that most of the heathland in the parish took the form of
'walks' attached to the largest farms, and only a relatively small proportion was

common land, exploited by the remainder of the tenants (IRO HA 24: 50/19/I.11). In some parishes even the smaller farms had diminutive parcels of private heath. In the parish of Reydon in 1697, for example, tenants like Nicholas Lisle held portions of less than two acres (IRO HA11: C2/10). Whether the heaths had already been occupied in this manner in the Middle Ages, or whether individual parcels like this were only allotted from the common in later times, remains unclear. Nevertheless, while much several heathland could be found, extensive areas of common heath did continue to exist throughout medieval and post-medieval times. We often hear about them when there were disputes over their use, as in 1385 when the Abbot of Sibton was indicted for overstocking the common at Westleton with sheep (he was acquitted: the jury found that rights to use the heath here had not been strictly apportioned) (Brown 1986, no. 11).

The uses of heathland

Heathland had many uses in the 'traditional' farming economy of medieval and early post-medieval times. It was only later agricultural 'improvers' who viewed it as useless waste. Furze (or gorse) was cut for fuel: it produces a rapid, intense heat suitable for kindling and bread ovens, and was the most common form of charcoal excavated at the Anglo-Saxon burial ground at Snape. It could also be used for fencing. John Norden, in his *Surveyor's Dialogue* of 1618,

FIGURE 25.
Bracken-dominated heath at Tunstall: bracken became a much more prominent constituent of the Sandlings heaths in the course of the later nineteenth and twentieth centuries.

thus described how the plant was employed 'to brew withall and bake, and to stoppe a little gap in a hedge' (Norden 1618, 234). Ling or heather was also used as fuel, and perhaps as thatch, and certain areas of heath may have been set apart for its cultivation and protected from grazing, as it was certainly sold in large quantities; at Staverton in 1305–06, sales raised £2 12s (Rackham 1986, 295). It was also used in farmyards, in place of straw, to judge from the diary of Samuel Gross, who farmed in the area in the 1840s (IRO SI/8/3.2). Bracken was also used for fuel and for thatch, but mainly as animal litter, and again its harvest could raise significant sums (fourteen shillings at Staverton in 1274–75) (Rackham 1986, 295). In addition, the turf could be stripped from the sheepwalks and used for domestic fires. Crabbe, writing in 'The Village', refers to the heath as a source of 'the light turf that warms the neighbouring poor' (Edwards 1991, 5).

While the heaths thus supplied a variety of produce for the local inhabitants their main use was always for grazing livestock, especially sheep. Although by post-medieval times cattle were in many ways the mainstay of the local farming economy, they were of less importance in the early Middle Ages, and in part this was because less land had yet been 'inned' from the salt marshes. While cattle could thrive on the alluvial marshes, they were less well suited to the heaths, for the thin grass and heather were less palatable to them than to sheep. Moreover, large areas of heathland were devoid of surface water, and cattle need to be watered more regularly than sheep. When in the middle of the thirteenth century Andrew Peverell granted the monks of Sibton Abbey the right to graze livestock on his heath at Nacton, the numbers were set at 240 sheep, but only seven cattle (Brown 1986, no. 265). Indeed, in spite of the importance of cattle in the local economy sheep continued to predominate on the Sandlings heaths up until the twentieth century, and some vast flocks are recorded – over a thousand on the Friston Hall estate in the 1690s, for example (Burrell 1960, 59).

Because the Sandlings heaths were so intensively grazed, less use could be made of the other 'crops', especially furze and gorse, than in some heathland districts. Norden, writing in 1618, noted that while in general he recommended the destruction of gorse, 'there is a kind of furze worth the preservation, if it grow in a Countrey barren of wood', and this supplied much of the fuel used in Devon and Cornwall. It grew 'very high, and the stalke great, whereof the people make faggots'. But he went on:

> And this kind of Furse groweth also upon the Sea coast of *Suffolke*. But that the people make not the use of them, as in *Devonshire* and *Cornwalle*, for they suffer their sheep and cattell to browse and crop them when they be young, and so they grow too scrubbed and lowe tufts, seldome to that perfection that they might be (Norden 1618, 235)

In the Sandlings, as in other areas of light soil in England, a form of sheep-corn husbandry was practised. Large flocks were grazed on the heaths by day, and close-folded by night on the arable fields, thus ensuring a constant flow of nutrients from the one to the other which allowed the poor, leached soils to be kept in heart (Kerridge 1967, 42–5). In the words of John Norden, who knew the Sandlings well, in light soil districts

> The farmers doe much enrich their Land indeede with the sheep-fold. A most easie, and a most profitable course; and who so neglecteth it, having means, may be condemned for an ill husband (Norden 1618, 229)

Not only the fallows, but also the newly-sown corn, might be folded, 'for the trampling of the sheepe, and their treading, doth settle the earth about the corne, keeping it the more moiste and warme, and causeth it to stand the faster' (Norden 1618, 229). In the far south of the district, where the heaths were most extensive, it was sometimes impractical to move the flock each night down on to the arable and folds were instead erected on the heath itself, and the dung collected and carted to the fields.

The heathland vegetation provided some nourishment even in the winter, when the grass growth in better pastures was meagre. In the worst weather the heather shoots would project above the snow (Armstrong 1973, 1). The adoption of turnips as a field crop in the eighteenth century lessened the importance of the heaths to some extent, providing as they did an alternative source of autumn and winter feed, but folding remained the cornerstone of Sandlings agriculture and leases often contain detailed prescriptions concerning the practice. One for Westwood Farm in Blythburgh, drawn up in the 1790s, thus ordered the tenant 'to keep at least 800 sheep and to fold them at all reasonable times in the year with the usual numbers of hurdles upon some part of the farm most likely to be benefited thereby', with a penalty of £5 for each night missed (IRO HA30/50/22/3.40). Moreover, even though folding in the fields on roots and green crops became a more important part of local farming, the heaths continued to play a significant role. In 1885 White was able to describe how 'close folding on the arable lands of the flock at night which has grazed or rather browsed on the heath land in the day, is the system chiefly relied upon for fertilising the arable lands' (White 1885, 55). Even in 1941 Butcher, while noting the importance of 'green crops and sugar beet tops in the autumn, and ... roots in the winter' as feed for the flocks, emphasised that they were 'run on the heaths and poor grassland in the summer' (Butcher 1941, 368).

Up until the nineteenth century the sheep grazed on the Sandlings heaths were of the traditional East Anglian breed, generally referred to as the 'Norfolk Horn'. They had mottled or black skins and long legs, and horns which were spiral in rams and straight in ewes and wethers. They were a hardy breed, well-adapted to folding, and in William Marshall's words could 'thrive upon open heath and barren sheep walks, where nine tenths of the breeds in the kingdom would starve' (Marshall 1787, 365). They produced sweet mutton, and short, fine fleeces (Kerridge 1967, 312). Across East Anglia as a whole this traditional breed was gradually replaced, in the course of the nineteenth century, by the South Down-Norfolk cross, also known as the Suffolk; but this process was slower in the Sandlings than in most other districts, and breeders would send here for rams when they needed to find fresh blood for their flocks (Wade Martins and Williamson 1999, 129).

Across large areas of Norfolk, Suffolk and Cambridgeshire the organisation of folding took a particular form, to which modern historians have given the name *fold course system* (Allison 1957; Bailey 1989). Folding arrangements were tightly controlled. While tenants might benefit from the manure dropped by the sheep as they roamed over the fallows, the intensive night-folding was the monopoly of the manorial lord. Tenants could usually only enjoy this in return for a cash payment. The sheep were organised into communal flocks, dominated by the stock of the lord (or his lessee), and under the care of a manorial shepherd. The grazing on large areas of heath, and often on any coastal marshes, was reserved to the demesne flock. Originally devised as a way of ensuring that the demesne arable received more than its fair share of manure, in post-medieval times the essence of the institution changed (Bailey 1990a). The fold course became a way of keeping large commercial flocks, from which lords or their lessees excluded the sheep of the tenants. Instead of monopolising the supplies of dung, in other words, lords now monopolised the meagre grazing supplied by the harvest aftermath and the fallow weeds on their tenants' arable land.

By the time documents become numerous, from the thirteenth century, the fold course was not as widespread in the Sandlings as it was in some other parts of East Anglia, most notably Breckland. In all probability it had never been such a well-established institution here, because there was much more good-quality pasture in the locality than in most other areas of light soil, especially on the coastal marshes, and there was thus less need to monopolise supplies of either manure or marginal grazing. But stray references show that such arrangements did exist in some parishes, even in the post-medieval period. In 1637 there was said to be two foldcourses in Blythburgh and Walberswick 'upon the sheepwalk or heath there, containing 500 acres' (IRO 50/22/3.1); while a sixteenth-century lease for Alderton refers to 'meadows, feedings, pastures, foldcourses …' (Burrell 1960, 34).

Many areas of heathland in the Sandlings were grazed not only by sheep, but also by rabbits, or coneys (often the same areas of heath were used for both). Rabbits are not indigenous to England but were introduced soon after the Norman Conquest, and were originally a semi-domesticated animal. By the fourteenth century large warrens were widespread in places where there were extensive areas of poor sandy soil – poor, that is, for crops, but ideal for burrowing animals. Rabbits were kept both for their fur and for their meat. In East Anglia the main concentrations of warrens were in Breckland and on the Sandlings. There were examples at Dunningworth (established by 1274), Iken (recorded from 1392), and within the deer park at Staverton (from *c.* 1322), while others are recorded at Blythburgh and Walberswick. Further examples were established in the course of the fifteenth, sixteenth and seventeenth centuries at Sutton, Shottisham, Staverton, Boyton, Levington,

Hollesley, Walton, Tunstall, Leiston, Covehithe and Westleton (Hoppitt 1999; Bailey 1988). The presence of others, of uncertain date, is indicated by minor place names on early maps, as at Bawdsey (IRO HD 11/47) or Levington (IRO HD 11/475). Rabbits continued to be farmed on a large scale right through the eighteenth and into the nineteenth century, and a number of new warrens were created: on the Rous estate, for example, 150 acres of former arable were converted to a warren in 1700 (IRO HA 11 L9/22). Rabbit farming gradually declined in importance through the late nineteenth century, largely because of the increased availability of other forms of cheap meat.

Warrens were sometimes operated directly by their owners but, in the post-medieval centuries especially, they were usually leased to professional warreners. Westwood Lodge Warren in Blythburgh, for example, was let for £15 *per annum* in 1690 (IRO HA 30: 50/22/3.43). The contract, drawn up between Sir Charles Blois and John Atkins, gave the latter all the 'Coneys or rabbits now being or remaining in and upon the lands', although Sir Charles reserved the right, when resident at Westwood Lodge, to 'have kill and take upon the said warren ... five couple of coneys every week from St James to Candlemass in every year'. Leases usually stipulated the number of rabbits which would be left on the warren at the end of the tenancy. At Nacton, for example, the tenant was to leave 'five hundred couple of coneys good, well conditioned and alive' when the lease expired in 1646 (IRO H93/3/48).

Whether managed directly or indirectly, warrens were a source of profit for their owners and operators. But they could also present them with problems. From an early date, poaching was widespread. Hungry peasants must have looked with envy at well-stocked warrens, but many convicted poachers came from more affluent sections of the community. In the early fifteenth century Augustinian canons from Blythburgh Priory were regularly convicted of rabbit poaching in the warren at Westwood near Dunwich. One, Thomas Sherman by name, was actually described in a court roll of 1425 as 'a poaching canon' (Bailey 1988, 17). In addition, escaped rabbits caused damage to crops, which could lead to prosecutions from neighbouring landowners. As early as 1392 a colony of rabbits at Iken – descendants of escapees from Dunningworth warren, some four kilometres to the east – was causing serious damage in the fields.

Considering the scale of the industry, rabbit farming has left few obvious traces in the landscape of the Sandlings. In some places the warrens were enclosed and subdivided with banks of turf, the remains of which survive in a number of places, as on Sutton Common. Elsewhere in England rabbits were regularly provided with low, ditched mounds, partly to encourage them to burrow but mainly to make their trapping – with nets and ferrets – easier. Archaeologists call them 'pillow mounds' but their traditional name – some-what confusingly – was 'berries' or 'burrows' (Loveday and Williamson 1988). They were less necessary where the soils were deep and sandy, as in the Sandlings, but they were sometimes constructed, probably as 'clappers' for breeding does, or when new warrens were first established on open heaths.

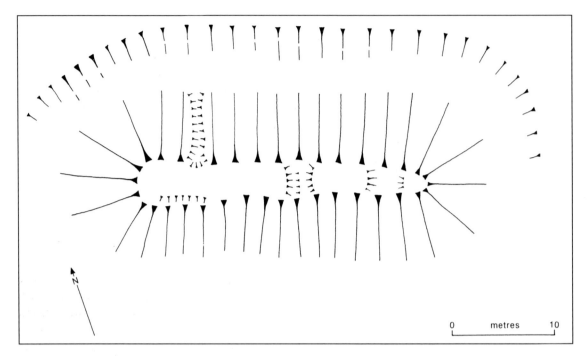

0   metres   10

FIGURE 26.
A 'pillow mound', relic of the post-medieval rabbit farming industry, on Sutton Common.

One can be seen on Sutton Common (TM31394765) – an abnormally large example, nearly two metres in height – set within a circular earthwork enclosure covering some 1.25 hectares, with which it is perhaps contemporary (Figure 26). Two smaller mound survive to the north, at TM31404806. Others examples remain at Nacton, and at Covehithe, where aerial photography has revealed further rectangular cropmarks which may represent the sites of other mounds, long destroyed (Hoppitt 1999). The existence of others, long since levelled, is indicated by post-medieval documents. A lease for Walberswick Warren, for example, drawn up in 1611, bound the tenant to 'make burrows for the said coneys' (IRO HA30: 50/22/1, 4). Sometimes existing earthworks, especially Bronze Age round barrows, may have been re-used as warren mounds, as, perhaps, at Stratton Hall (TM251392: Suffolk County Council Historic Environment Record).

The various ways in which the heaths were used in the medieval and early post-medieval periods ensured that they would have had a more managed appearance, and a rather different pattern of vegetation, than that first recorded by nineteenth- and twentieth-century ecologists. As already noted, intensive grazing would have ensured that the heather was much more closely cropped than it normally is today. Grass was almost certainly more prominent on what are now purely heather heaths, since grazing and regular cutting for fuel would have reduced the dominance of both heather and gorse, allowing *Festuca ovina, Agrostis tenuis* and other grasses to flourish. In addition, periodic ploughing of parts of the heaths, in order to take cereal crops for a few years – a widespread practice, as we shall see – tended to favour grass over other heathland plants (Kerridge 1967, 79). Many heaths which now carry a near-continuous cover of heather were thus probably more of a patchwork of grass and heather. Nevertheless, large areas of continuous heather probably always existed, especially where the heaths were most extensive. Norden, talking about 'sandie, hot grounds' where heather dominated the landscape, drew particular attention to the area between '*Wilford Bridge*, and *Snape Bridge*, in Suffolke' (Norden 1618, 233). Above all, regular grazing tended to reduce the extent of invasion by bracken, shrubs and trees: bracken would have been much rarer than today and although seventeenth-century maps do show some trees, and scatters of thorn bushes, across certain of the larger heaths, most seem to have been almost entirely treeless (Figure 27).

The extent and decline of the heaths

The frontier of arable cultivation tended to expand at the expense of heath as population rose during the twelfth and thirteenth centuries. When, in the early thirteenth century, the monks of Sibton Abbey were granted rights to pasture their stock on Nacton Heath, the grantee excluded 'the land newly broken into cultivation or otherwise converted' (Brown 1986, no. 265). But by the mid thirteenth century, and in some places before this date, a point of rough equilibrium seems to have been reached. The expansion of arable slowed, or stopped, in part because the remaining areas of heathland were on soils so poor that they could not be cultivated economically on a permanent basis; and in part because such heathland as remained was necessary for the sustenance of the flocks, without which insufficient dung would be available for maintaining the fertility of the arable land.

It is important to emphasise that since the thirteenth century heathland only ever occupied a minority of the land area in Sandlings parishes, even those located on the very worst soils in the south of the district. The survey of the Stanhope estates in Iken, Sudbourne, Wantisden, Chillesford and neighbouring parishes, for example, made by John Norden in *c.* 1601, clearly shows that while heaths were certainly extensive the arable land occupied a far greater area (IRO V5/22/1; EE5/11/1). In Sutton, surveyed in 1629, the situation was similar, with heaths accounting for little more than a third of the total land area (IRO JA1/54/182). But we must also be careful not to posit too sharp or simple a dichotomy between the permanent arable on the one hand and the permanent heaths and sheepwalks on the other. In practice, especially in times of rising population and rising prices, portions of heath would be broken up and cultivated for a time, before being allowed to tumble back to furze and ling. In a court case held in 1637 it was claimed that the lord of the manor of Blythburgh and Walberswick, or his demesne farmer:

> Used to plow such parte of the said walke or heath as they would; &
> when any part thereof was sowen with corne, the inhabitants of
> Walberswick did not put their cattle upon such places soe sowen untill
> the corne was reaped, but if their cattle did stray & come on the corne

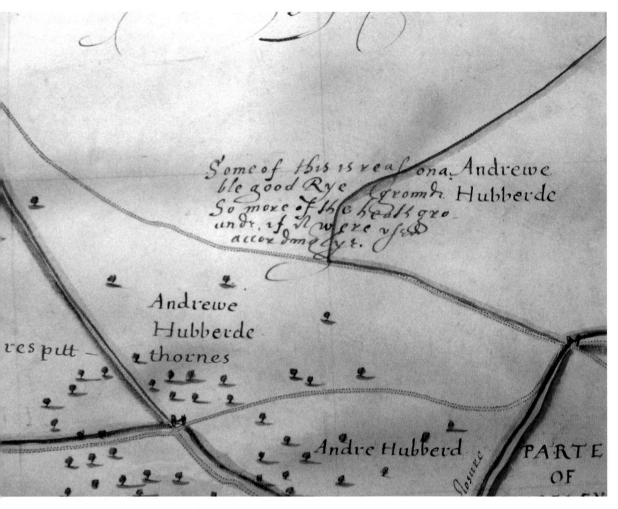

Some of this is reasona-
ble good Rye Andrewe
So more of the heath gro- Hubberde
under, if it were used
accordingly.

respitt

Andrewe
Hubberde
thornes

Andre Hubberd

PARTE
OF

they were impounded. And that it appearses by the rigges and furrowes
on most parte of the heath, that the same have usually byn ploughed
(IRO HA 30: 50/22/3.1)

On several of Norden's maps of the Stanhope estates in Sudbourne,
Wantisden and the surrounding parishes, annotations indicate the periodic use
of the heaths as arable. One area in Chillesford was described as being 'heathye
and barren yet in some places beareth indifferent good rye' (IRO EE5/11/1):
while of another, to the south-east of Staverton, Norden noted: 'some of this
is reasonable good rye ground; so more of the heath grounde if it were used
accordingly' (IRO V5/22/1). Such cultivation (especially of private heaths)
continued into the eighteenth century. Crabbe, in 'The Village', thus
described how, in the midst of the heaths, 'a length of burning sand appears'

Where the thin harvest waves its withered ears;
Rank weeds, that every art and care defy,
Reign o'er the land, and rob the blighted rye (Edwards 1991, 5)

FIGURE 27.
Extract from John
Norden's survey of the
Stanhope estates,
1600–01, showing
heathland in the south
east of Bromeswell.
Note the scatter of
thorn, a relatively
unusual feature, and
Norden's comments
about the cultivation of
rye on the heath.

As late as 1885 White's Directory noted how 'such lands, the better spots at least, are occasionally broken up and cultivated for a few years, and then laid down again on a self-sown herbage for a ten, twenty or perhaps a thirty year rest' (White 1885, 4).

Shifting cultivation was thus a feature of the heaths throughout the post-medieval period. But the later eighteenth century saw a further development. As the price of grain rose steadily, areas of heathland began to be cultivated on a more regular basis – they began to be permanently reclaimed. In 1784 the Frenchman Francois de la Rochefoucauld, travelling through Sutton, described how

> It is in the past twenty years or so that all this countryside – perhaps twenty square miles – has been inhabited. The extreme depth of the shifting sand had until then defeated the reclaimers ... I saw some very fine crops in land that – simply judged by someone who will not make a perfect connoisseur of soil – one would suppose could produce nothing. An acre is rented at five or six shillings a year ... (Scarfe 1988a, 135)

Arthur Young, in 1795, similarly described the recent changes made on the 'extensive wastes of Sutton':

> Having long ago called on the farmers publicly to cultivate them, I cannot but recollect the answers I then received – that it would not answer – and that they were fit only for what they gave – coarse sheepwalk. I have now the pleasure to find my old opinion confirmed, for great tracts have been broken up within these twenty years, and are found to answer well ... (Young 1795, 38)

The scale of reclamation probably intensified as the Napoleonic War blockade pushed grain prices to unprecedented levels, and where the heaths were common land they were sometimes enclosed by parliamentary act in this period, like the 233 acres of waste enclosed in Foxhall in 1804, or the 501 acres of 'heaths, plains, commons and waste grounds' divided in the same year at Bucklesham (Wade Martins and Williamson 1999, 44).

Large-scale conversion of heathland to arable was only possible if the severe acidity of the soils could be ameliorated. Cereal yields are badly affected by soil acidity, especially those of barley. But in addition, it was difficult to adopt the new 'improved' rotations of the eighteenth century on such 'sour' soils, for turnips are liable to fail completely in acid conditions and are prone to attack by finger-and-toe disease (Hanley 1949, Vol 1, 138; Robinson 1949, 232). Moreover, reclaimed land could soon become overrun again with bracken and other heathland vegetation, if the soil was left in its natural condition. In Norden's words:

> It is the nature of Furze, Broome, and Brakes, to keepe their standing, and hardly will yeelde the possession once gotten in a field: for commonly they like the soyle well, and the soyle them; and where there is a mutuall congruity, there is seldome a voluntary separation.

And therefore, as long as there is not a disturbance of their possession with a contrary earth, they will keepe where they are ... And therefore as the soyle is commonly barren, hot and dry where they live, make this ground fat and fruitful, and they will die. And therefore the greatest enemy that may be set to encounter them is good and rich Marle, and thereupon, the plough some few yeares together, and you shall see, they will shrinke away, and hide their heads (Norden 1618, 239)

As Norden describes, the principal method of remedying soil acidity was to mix the sandy soil with some kind of calcareous material, excavated from the subsoil or brought in from another district. Pockets of calcareous clay or *marl*, of glacial origin, occur sporadically in the sandy drift, and these could be excavated and spread upon the land, and as early as 1601 there are references to treating land with lime made from shells collected from the sea shore. The most important remedy for acidity, however, was a particular form of crag – an especially shelly, calcareous variety which occurs at no great depth, especially in the area to the east of Woodbridge, and which could be excavated from pits and spread on the surface with relative ease. Kirby believed that crag had first been used in 1718 by a farmer in Levington, but there is little doubt that the practice had been known long before this (Kirby 1735, 84). Norden shows a number of pits on his map of the Stanhope estates surveyed in 1600–01, one lying in a close called 'Marlingfield' (IRO V5/22/1); these were almost certainly dug to extract crag rather than any other calcareous material. Either way, the practice certainly increased in the course of the eighteenth century, and in the 1790s Arthur Young described how, in the area around Ramsholt, 'pits are to be seen on every farm, some very large and deep' (Young 1797, 130). Crag pits are still a common sight in this part of the Sandlings (Figures 28 and 29). The pits could be dangerous places. In October 1808 one James Harding was killed in Sutton due to the collapse of a pit 'situate in a field called Crag Pit Hill' (HB10: 50/20/9.14).

Crag, marl, and other calcareous earths were applied to existing fields, as well as to intakes from the heath, for most agricultural land in this part of Suffolk is to some extent acidic. But it was in the reclamation of the very poorest lands, occupied by the heaths, that the use of these materials was most intensive, and most indispensable. In the 1735 edition of John Kirby's *The Suffolk Traveller* it was estimated that around a third of the 'Sandlands' was occupied by heaths and sheepwalks; but the 1829 edition of the book stated that 'many hundred acres of them are now converted into good arable land by that excellent manure' (Kirby 1735, 2; 1829, 3). In the words of John Glyde, writing in 1856, 'The admixture of the subsoil with the surface has contributed more than anything else to place the cultivation of the light lands of Suffolk in the first rank in the scale of farming (Glyde 1856, 10).

In many places, however – and especially towards the north of the district – 'calcareous earths' were not locally available, and soil acidity remained a serious problem. Young described how chalk was brought from Essex and

Kent in empty cornhoys returning from London (Young 1797, 137). Some farmers carted calcareous clay many miles from the claylands to the west, but this was an expensive operation; in the neighbourhood of Wrentham it was reported in 1849 that 'Marling is but little done in this locality, by reason of the distance it has to be brought' (Raynbird and Raynbird 1849, 133). In 1824 the agent of the Middleton estate wrote of the Denham Bridge farm near Ipswich that 'there being no clay or heavy earth to be obtained, prevent the improvement of this light soil', while on a farm in Nacton he reported that:

> Lands of this description have felt a greater depression than the fair mixed soil. There is a great uncertainty of crop, for want of fresh earth or clay the layers will not stand well, even for one year' (IRO HA 93: 3/155)

The limited supply of suitable 'calcareous earths' may well be one of the reasons why the extent of heathland reclamation in the Sandlings in the late eighteenth and nineteenth centuries was, perhaps, rather less than the enthusiastic outpourings of Young and Rochefoucauld might lead us to believe. A paucity of good-quality maps from the period before the eighteenth century makes the progress of reclamation hard to chart with any accuracy, while maps of all periods (even the Ordnance Survey six inch maps of the late nineteenth and early twentieth centuries) are often ambiguous in their classification of land use. Indeed, in reality the line between 'pasture', 'rough grazing', 'sheepwalk' and 'heath' was always vague and uncertain. Bearing all this in mind, a comparison of the extent of heath and sheepwalk shown on Norden's 1600–01 survey of the Stanhope estates (IRO V5/22/1; EE5/11/1) with that depicted on the Tithe Award maps of *c.* 1840 (Figure 30), suggests that while a significant reduction occurred in some places (to the south-east of Tunstall, for example, or across large parts of Sudbourne) elsewhere only relatively limited inroads were made into the heaths, and some areas which were arable in the seventeenth century had actually become heath by the nineteenth. Certainly, vast areas of heathland remained to be reclaimed in the mid nineteenth century. Comparison of the Tithe Award maps and the First and Second Edition Ordnance Survey maps from the late nineteenth and early twentieth centuries suggest little further expansion of the frontiers of cultivation during the Victorian 'high farming' period (Figure 30).

Even where heavy applications of 'calcareous earths' were economic, or possible, these could do little to remedy the extreme droughtiness of the soils, or their deficiency in key chemicals like boron and manganese. Moreover, the extent to which arable could expand at the expense of heathland was limited by the need to keep particularly large flocks of sheep, in order to maintain the fertility of the poor soils: even with the widespread adoption of turnips as a field crop, additional forms of grazing were required, especially in the winter. An early nineteenth-century survey of a farm at Denham Bridge near Ipswich thus criticised the extent of the arable land: 'The absence of heath prevents the most being made of the arable, which is extremely light, poor and uncertain land. The more sheep an occupation can keep the better as the land is more adapted to them than corn. If 50–100 acres of heath could be added to this farm, I would consider it very desirable' (IRO HA 12: 3/155). Even where the heaths were destroyed, large areas of the 'improved' land often remained under pasture, and might then be subject to renewed invasion by bracken and gorse. Arable rotations, too, frequently featured long grass 'leys'. A lease of 1803 for a farm in Nacton, for example, laid down a 6-course shift for 100 acres of the land. Under this system a sixth of the land was under turnips, a sixth was sown with barley or oats and the rest was 'layer'; that is, sown with grass or clover (IRO HA 93: 3/208). A survey of farms on the Saumarez estates, made in 1809, urged how on Bryants Farm near Ipswich 'The heath enclosures [should] be kept in layer which will enable the tenant to keep more sheep for the improvement of the enclosed lands' (IRO HA 12:3/155).

FIGURE 28.
A particularly large example of a crag pit at Chillesford.

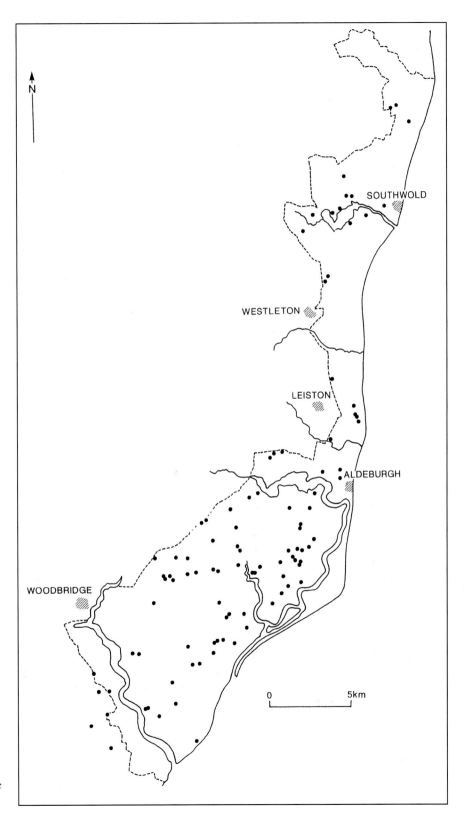

FIGURE 29.
The distribution of
crag and marling pits
in the Sandlings (only
pits probably dug for
the extraction of
'calcareous earths' have
been included).

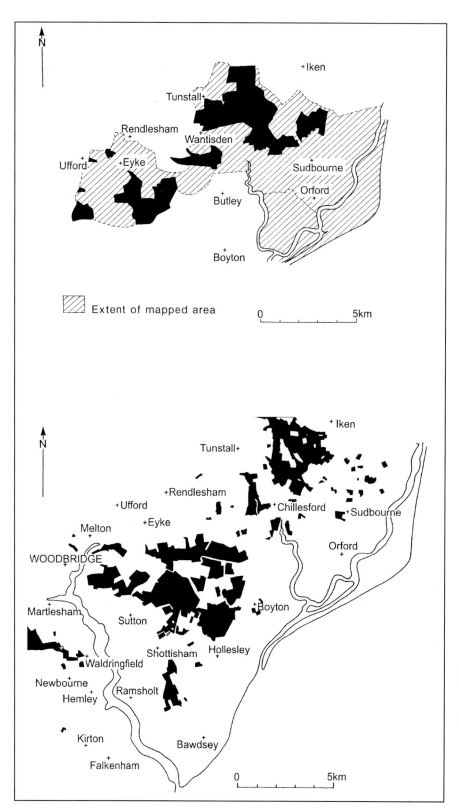

Extent of mapped area

0   5km

0   5km

FIGURE 30.
left and opposite
The distribution of
heathland in the
southern Sandlings.
Top left: areas of
heathland and 'walks'
shown on John
Norden's survey of the
Stanhope estates,
1600–01. Below left:
distribution of
heathland shown on
the Tithe Award maps,
c. 1840. Top right: areas
of heathland and rough
grazing shown on the
second edition
Ordnance Survey maps,
1905. Below right:
distribution of
heathland recorded by
the Land Utilisation
Survey in 1935.

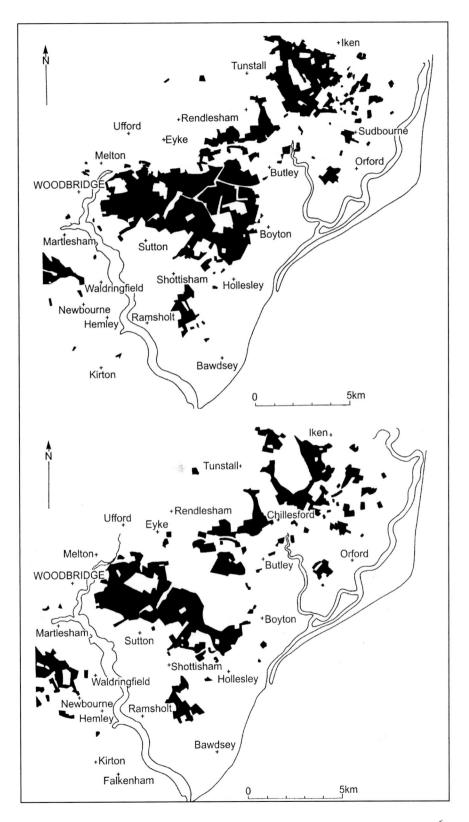

The extent to which heaths were converted to arable land in the agricultural revolution period was thus relatively limited, especially when compared with the scale of reclamation in other heathland areas of East Anglia, such as north-west Norfolk. Moreover, some of the land that *was* reclaimed gradually reverted to heath once more during the agricultural recession of the late nineteenth and early twentieth centuries. As grain prices plummeted, it was simply uneconomical to farm such marginal land. The Acquisition Reports drawn up by the Forestry Commission, prior to the purchase of properties for afforestation in the 1920s and 30s, refer on a number of occasions to areas of derelict arable. One from 1938, relating to land owned by the Campsea Ashe estate in Tunstall, states that:

> The land under review consists mainly of arable fields which have been lying derelict for 2, 3, or 4 years, although a small part is still in cultivation ... The small patches of rough land which have been lying idle for several years carry a fairly strong growth of bracken with some bramble, broom, privet, lichen and carex grass. On the land which has been more recently in cultivation carex and bracken is beginning to appear and these fields carry for the most part fine grasses with traces of ragwort and lichen. There is a little gorse to be seen here and there ... Some of the land has been cultivated from Game feed purposes and other fields have been relinquished by the Estate tenants owing to a reduction in the size of their farms. The owner's agents see no hope of the land under review being maintained under agriculture (Forestry Commission archives, Santon Downham, uncatalogued)

The Land Utilisation Survey of 1941 estimated that there were some 890 acres of 'derelict arable land' in eastern Suffolk, compared with over 15,000 acres of land classified as 'heathland' (Butcher 1941, Appendix II). Most of the latter had probably never been converted to permanent arable, but some may have been reclaimed land which had by this time been abandoned for so long that it had acquired a ground cover indistinguishable from that of the neighbouring heaths.

More important were the effects of the agricultural recession upon the *character* of the heaths. In the 1920s and 30s the numbers of sheep kept in the district declined markedly (Trist 1971, 103, 110; Armstrong 1973). This was partly because of the low prices which could be obtained for lamb; partly because the numbers of cattle were increasing on local farms (a change which was itself, in part, associated with the adoption of sugar beet as a major crop in the district in the 1920s); and partly because of the high labour costs involved in erecting folds, and the difficulties in obtaining experienced shepherds (Armstrong 1973). In consequence, the heaths were now less intensively grazed than before. Ecological changes soon followed. White described in 1885 how the heaths were 'covered with a short velvety herbage of grass or moss and studded more or less with furze bushes. In other places it is completely covered with ling or heather. Sheep readily browse the young shoots of the furze and eat the early grass, but if either gets beyond a few inches in length, neither the one nor the other is usable for sheep's feed' (White 1885, 20). The reduction in stocking levels thus began a downward spiral, leading both to an increase in the height and quantity of heather, and to the invasion of bracken: changes to which the decline in the numbers of rabbit warrens also contributed. Hawthorn, sloe, and birch soon appeared and, in places, Scots pine, invading from adjacent plantations. Once again, the Forestry Commission Acquisition Reports from the 1920s and 30s make the derelict condition of the heaths very clear. That for Iken Heath, for example, drawn up in 1920, describes the 'very strong growths of heather, bracken etc with gorse and thorn bushes and a number of pine groups in scattered form' (Forestry Commission Archives, Santon Downham, uncatalogued).

One immediate consequence of recession, and of the redundancy and dereliction of the heaths, was an increase in the area under plantations: a number of local landowners in the 1880s and 1890s saw forestry as a good alternative use for this marginal land. But, as we shall see, it was with the arrival on the scene of the Forestry Commission in the 1920s and 30s that really extensive areas of heathland disappeared under trees (below, pages 111–14), radically changing both the appearance and the ecology of large areas of the Sandlings.

Although vast areas of open heathland survived into the second half of the twentieth century, especially in the south of the district, it was thus in an increasingly derelict state. Then, with a return of agricultural prosperity and major improvements in farming technology, the heaths really came under sustained attack. Small-scale attempts at reclamation had been made in the 1920s, and again in the 1940s (Trist 1971, 120). But it was only from 1949 that very large areas were ploughed, a development fuelled by government subsidies for ploughing and liming, by widespread use of artificial fertilisers, and by the availability of cheap chemical treatments to rectify potash, boron, manganese and copper deficiencies in the soil (Trist 1971, 120–3; Armstrong 1973). Irrigation was first adopted in the area in 1947 (the farmer in question was the first in England to use this new technology), spread quite rapidly during the 1950s and was practised on a significant scale by the end of the 1960s, boosting yields and making it possible to grow potatoes even on the worst soils (Trist 1971, 124).

The most extensive reclamations were in the south of the district, where the area of heathland – especially private heathland – had always been greatest. Between 1949 and 1952, 1,533 acres (620 hectares) were ploughed at Wantisden Hall, at Iken Hall, at Lodge Farm in Sudbourne and on the Shottisham, Martlesham, and Waldringfield Heaths. By 1955 a further 1,120 acres (453 hectares) had been reclaimed around Sutton Hoo and on Sutton Common, at Methersgate Hall, and on the Kesgrave, Bromeswell, Hollesley, Nacton and Brightwell Heaths. The years between 1955 and 1964 saw a further 207 acres (84 hectares) ploughed in Shottisham, Sutton and Hollesley. There were also

FIGURE 31.
overleaf
The reduction of heathland in the Sandlings, 1905–*c.* 2000 (based on the Ordnance Survey maps).

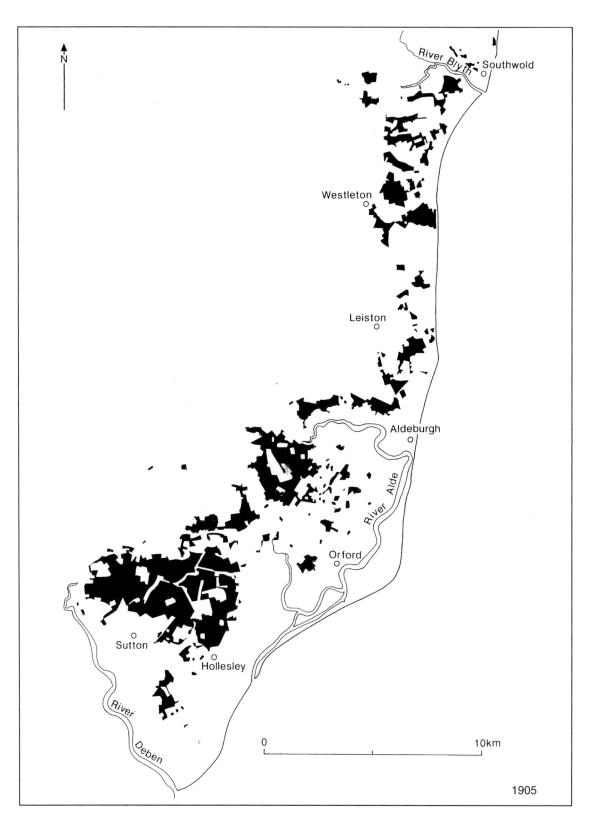

N

River Blyth

Southwold

Westleton

Leiston

Aldeburgh

River Alde

Orford

Sutton

Hollesley

River

Deben

0   10km

1905

72

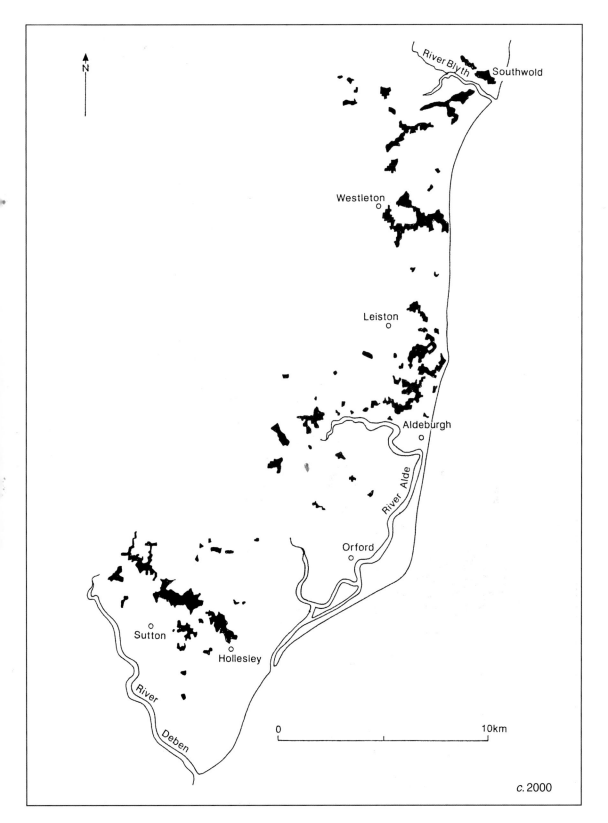

N

River Blyth

Southwold

Westleton

Leiston

Aldeburgh

River Alde

Orford

Sutton

Hollesley

River

Deben

0   10km

c. 2000

some losses further north, with some 490 acres (198 hectares) being brought into cultivation in the 1950s in Walberswick, Dunwich, Leiston, Aldringham and Snape, together with 130 acres (53 hectares) on the Benacre estate. In all, some 3,640 acres (1,473 hectares) of heathland were lost to agriculture in the Sandlings between 1949 and 1970 (Trist 1971, 121).

Reclamation was an arduous business, more difficult in some ways than it had been in the eighteenth and nineteenth centuries due to the overgrown and derelict condition of the heathland. Much of the heather had grown into 'tough woody plants standing up to 2 foot in height' (Trist 1971, 122). In the first reclamations, in the late 1940s and 50s, the heather and bracken were first burnt and then ploughed, to a depth of ten inches, with a single furrow digger plough. Ten or twenty tons of chalk were then applied per acre. Where the heather had grown especially high, a rotary cultivator was used to break down the plants and a second dressing, of ten tons of chalk per acre, was applied.

FIGURE 32.
Tunstall Common, showing the mixture of open heather, with areas of scrub and woodland, which is now typical of many Sandlings heaths.

The heather did not easily break down, however, in spite of repeated cultivations, and the chalk was often applied in lump form, as well as finely ground, and was sometimes distributed unevenly from the backs of lorries, leading to areas of uncorrected acidity (Trist 1971, 122–3). From the late 1950s forage harvesters were employed to clear the heather, and the chalk was applied in more finely ground form, carefully ploughed in, and then added as a surface dressing. Additionally, deep ploughing, to destroy the podzols of iron and humus to a depth of 0.3–1.0 metres, was often necessary.

The expansion of arable was only one threat which faced the heaths in the course of the twentieth century. Vast areas also disappeared under airfields – more than 500 hectares were swallowed up by Martlesham, Woodbridge and Bentwaters; under housing and golf courses; and, in particular, beneath the new Forestry Commission plantations and through regeneration to woodland. All in all, between 1889 and 1966 the area of open heathland in the Sandlings was reduced from around 7,700 hectares to around 3,400 (Armstrong 1973, 5–6). The last decades of the twentieth century saw further losses, partly to agriculture and housing but largely through regeneration to woodland, a process encouraged by the decline in the rabbit population following the onset of myxomatosis in 1953 (Armstrong 1973, 6).

By the end of the century the area of heathland along the Suffolk coast had thus been drastically reduced (Figure 31). That which remained, moreover, was in real danger of 'bushing over'. Fortunately, a number of important initiatives – the Suffolk Biodiversity Action Plan, the Sandlings Walks Project – and the activities of such bodies as the Sandlings Group, the RSPB and the Suffolk Wildlife Trust have begun to reverse the decline. New areas of heathland have been created, and over 400 hectares of heath are now being grazed once again – an astounding achievement, only possible through the erection of nearly 17 kilometres of sheep-proof fencing. After a century or more of destruction and degeneration, the outlook for the Sandlings heaths is now beginning to look much more promising (Figure 32).

CHAPTER FOUR

Settlements, Fields and Boundaries

Village and farmstead

Heaths, fens and marshes are the most noticeable elements of the Sandlings landscape. But large parts of the district are occupied by a more 'normal' countryside, of villages, farms and fields. This also has its own unique history: and the forms of settlements, the kinds of buildings they contain, the shape of fields and the character of the hedges that surround them all add to the rich tapestry of the district's distinctive landscape. Perhaps the most obvious feature is the character of local settlement. There are numerous nucleated villages but also, away from the more extensive areas of heath or former heath, a plethora of smaller places – outlying farms and cottages, and small hamlets. Early maps leave no doubt that, before the eighteenth century, such scattered settlements were even more numerous, and villages rather less prominent (Figure 33). How, and why, did this distinctive settlement pattern emerge?

Field-walking surveys, most notably that carried out by John Newman, have shown that here (as elsewhere in England) early Saxon settlements were generally small, often occupied only for a short period of time, and usually quite mobile; farms tended to drift across the landscape (Hamerow 1991; Newman 1993). From the seventh and eighth centuries settlement stabilised, often at places now marked in the landscape by villages and parish churches. In addition, however, there were also other, subsidiary settlements in the Saxon landscape. Domesday mentions several examples, some of which can be identified with medieval manors or with modern farms and hamlets, such as *Kenebroc*, now Kembroke Hall in Bucklesham, or *Candelenta*, Candlet Farm in Trimley (Scarfe 1988b). The locations of others, such as *Mycelgata* or *Hopewella* in Colneis Hundred, remain unknown or uncertain. Some of these places, like Hinton or Bulcamp in Blythburgh, continued as significant hamlets into modern times, but many remained as, or declined to the status of, single farms or 'halls'. Other small settlements existed in 1086 which are not mentioned by Domesday, which was concerned with units of administration and property – vills and manors – rather than with settlements *per se*. Probable examples include Sizewell and Thorpe near Aldringham. Indeed, even places which later came to be quite substantial parishes, such as Friston or Hazelwood, are passed over in silence by Domesday, although they almost certainly existed, in these particular cases included within the territory of Aldeburgh.

The density of separately-named Domesday settlements increases markedly towards the south of the Sandlings. Quite why this should be so is uncertain, but may be connected with the early economic and political importance of the district around Sutton Hoo and Rendlesham. Many of these places were mentioned because they were independent landholdings, occupied by free men; perhaps the lineal descendants of the kin groups who had formed the core of middle Saxon society, and who were thick on the ground in this area, close to the centres of political power. By the time of Domesday the holdings of such individuals had often become minutely subdivided so that, for example, the 319 acres which Domesday records in Capel were held by no fewer than 41 free men (with the exception of twelve acres belonging to the church). Most of these middle and later Saxon sites – whether marked today by modern villages, or by small farms and isolated hamlets – are located close to good supplies of water: beside rivers and major streams or, in the south of the region, at the springline which occurs at the boundary between the London clay and the overlying sand and gravels.

Across much of the district the pattern of settlement was thus fairly scattered by the time of the Norman Conquest. Further developments increased the extent of dispersion. From late Saxon times, and continuing through the twelfth and thirteenth centuries, farms and cottages began to spread away from the old sites. Sometimes they congregated on the edges of greens and commons – especially the damp 'low' commons beside streams and rivers. Elsewhere they were simply strung out along roadsides and tracks leading through the fields (Martin 2001). In some places the attraction of these new sites was so strong that farms moved away wholesale, leaving churches alone or virtually alone in the fields, as at Reydon, Snape, Aldringham, Butley or Benacre. Sometimes these changes led to the emergence of large, sprawling settlements: where farms clustered around a network of closely-spaced small commons, as at Southwold; or where, as at Westleton, farms congregated around what became a single large 'village green' (Figure 34). But for the most part the drift and expansion of settlement in early medieval times produced a loose scatter of single farms and isolated cottages, on roadsides, around small greens, or along the margins of fens and heaths.

A further layer of dispersal seems to have been added in the course of the fifteenth, sixteenth and seventeenth centuries. As we shall see, this period saw the gradual enclosure of the open fields that had formerly occupied most of the better land in the district. As holdings were consolidated, farms were sometimes erected on new and convenient sites. Certainly, many examples shown on early maps of the area stand within fields which, judging from their shape, had been created through the early enclosure of open arable.

The medieval Sandlings shared its dispersed settlement pattern with a much wider tract of countryside, extending across most of Norfolk and Suffolk, and southwards and westwards into Essex and Hertfordshire (Williamson 2003, 91–120). Historians and archaeologists continue to argue about why areas like this came to be characterised by scattered settlements while, in the Midlands,

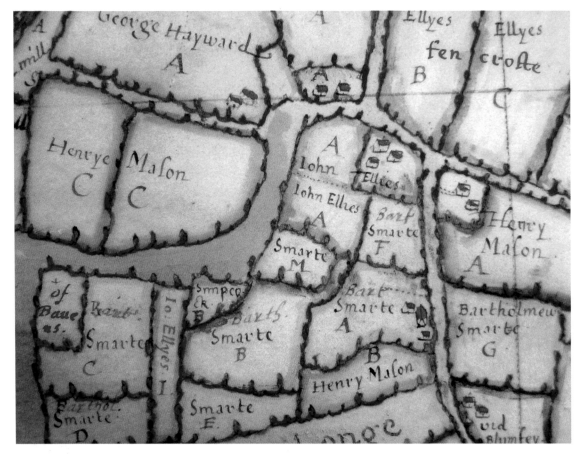

most medieval farmers lived in strongly-nucleated villages (Lewis, Mitchell-Fox and Dyer 2002). In part the answer may lie in environmental factors. In the Midlands, medieval peasants combining together to form plough teams – to till their own or their lord's land – were obliged to dwell in close proximity because the heavy, intractable soils could only be cultivated (especially in spring) over a short period of time, when the weather was favourable. Ploughing such land when wet caused 'puddling' and compaction. Plough oxen needed to be assembled rapidly, whenever a window of opportunity presented itself, and it thus made sense for farmers to dwell close together, rather than in farms scattered across the landscape (Williamson 2003, 141–59). In East Anglia, in contrast, the drier climate and more tractable character of the soils – especially in areas like the Sandlings – made such clustering of dwellings less necessary. In addition to this, Midland communities enjoyed extensive reserves of hay meadow associated with the wide alluvial valleys of the rivers Nene, Ouse, Welland and their tributaries (Williamson 2003, 160–79). A strong dependence on hay also ensured a clustering of settlement, for the 'window of opportunity' available for cutting, turning and stacking the mown grass was again a short one: 'make hay while the sun shines'. Farmers and labourers needed to live close together, at no great distance from this important resource, so that every advantage could be taken of weather conditions suitable for harvesting and haymaking. In northern and eastern East Anglia, in contrast, the character of soils and topography – valleys filled with wet peat rather than alluvial soils – ensured that hay meadows were developed rather later than in the Midlands, and were always in limited supply, relative to the area's population density. This meant that the clustering of farms in nucleated villages was less necessary; it may also have ensured that larger areas of common pasture were kept, so that livestock could be grazed late into the year, and that farms were attracted to their margins in order to exploit them conveniently (Williamson 2003, 176–8).

Historians and geographers often write as if settlement patterns, once established in the early middle ages, remained relatively unchanged into the modern period (e.g. Roberts and Wrathmell 2002). In reality, the pattern and morphology of villages, farms and hamlets continued everywhere to develop in response to changes in population, in the agrarian economy, and in patterns of landholding. The period of demographic decline in the fifteenth and early sixteenth centuries led to some contraction of settlement in the Sandlings, and

FIGURE 34.
The village green at Westleton.

some small villages were reduced to the status of minor hamlets, like Dunningworth in Tunstall. But at least as dramatic were the changes which took place in the course of the seventeenth, eighteenth and nineteenth centuries. As already noted, early seventeenth-century maps invariably show a more scattered pattern of settlement than that which exists in the district today, with farms and cottages standing on sites now empty of dwellings. In the parish of Sutton, for example, no fewer than ten outlying farms and isolated cottages seem to have disappeared from the landscape between the early seventeenth and the late nineteenth century: one or two new ones appeared, it is true, but the overall trend is clear enough.

What is also interesting is that in the same general period nucleated settlements – villages – became a more noticeable feature, especially in the south of the district. In 1631 Shottisham church stood almost alone, accompanied only by a farm and three cottages, with a further three houses loosely strung out along the road approaching from the east (IRO JA1/54 (1)). By the end of the nineteenth century this loose collection of dwellings had developed into a substantial village, with school and public house; over the same period, several outlying farmsteads in the parish were abandoned. Sudbourne village is a tight cluster of houses of eighteenth- and nineteenth-century date around a cross-roads a kilometre to the north-west of Sudbourne church. But until the early nineteenth century this settlement hardly existed. Instead, the area comprised a large common – Sudbourne Common – divided into two by a north–south road and a narrow strip of enclosed ground, probably a post-medieval encroachment (Figure 35). A dozen or so farms and cottages were scattered around its margins. In 1807 the common was enclosed by parliamentary act and was divided between the principal proprietors, the Marquis of Hertford receiving the lion's share (IRO HB 83 1379). New east–west roads were laid out and the existing north–south road straightened. By the start of the twentieth century a Baptist chapel, school and a number of new houses had appeared: since then, a nucleated 'village' has emerged.

Expansion of cultivation in the later eighteenth and nineteenth centuries occasionally led to the creation of new farms in intakes from the heath, but for the most part the development of settlement in the post-medieval period was dominated by a reduction in the number of isolated dwellings, and the emergence of larger, and more strongly nucleated, villages. Almost certainly, these changes were associated, at least in part, with the growth and consolidation of large landed estates, and the concomitant growth in the size of tenanted holdings, which rendered redundant many of the farms located in the less convenient and more isolated locations.

It should, however, be emphasised that not every parish in the Sandlings was owned, in its entirety, by a large estate. Some smaller proprietors remained in the area, in villages lying in the interstices between the larger blocks of property. Both modern historians, and contemporaries, have used the terms 'open' and 'closed' to characterise these two broad types of parish in eighteenth- and nineteenth-century England (Holderness 1972). Open parishes, which had larger numbers of landowners, tended to grow in size, acquire more facilities, and usually came to possess at least one nonconformist meeting place. In closed parishes, in contrast, a single owner (or two large owners) limited the population in order to keep down the Poor Rates; restricted the development of shops and, in particular, alehouses; and forbade the erection of non-conformist chapels and meeting houses. Some historians have criticised this simple model, and even a cursory examination of the Sandlings suggests that the connections between patterns of land ownership and the character of eighteenth- and nineteenth-century settlements were probably more complex than it suggests (Banks 1988).

Some local villages certainly fit the model well. Benacre, for example, was clearly a parish of 'closed' type. Owned in its entirety by the Gooch family, in 1881 it had a population density of only 32 individuals per square kilometre. The family resided in Benacre Hall and in 1885, according to White's *Directory*, there was a single shop and no places of worship other than the parish church (White 1885, 122–3). The adjacent parish of South Cove, also owned by the Gooch family, likewise had a population density of around 32 people per square kilometre and again possessed no shops or chapels, although it did have a public house, the Five Bells (White 1885, 223; Glyde 1856, 326). The neighbouring parishes of Wrentham and Kessingland, in contrast, were in diverse ownership. They contained numerous shops in the 1880s, and had two pubs each. Kessingland had a Wesleyan chapel, Wrentham both an Independent meeting house and a Primitive Methodist chapel (White 1885, 673–4, 445–6). Moreover, while they embraced very similar soils to Benacre and South Cove, they had much denser populations, with 184 and 105 individuals per square kilometre respectively. The contrast between these two groups of parishes is still very evident. Benacre and South Cove remain small places with no facilities; Wrentham and Kessingland are large and bustling, and still have their nonconformist chapels (the Independent meeting at Wrentham, now Congregationalist, is a particularly fine building of 1778). Several other parishes towards the north of the district were similar in character, notably Theberton and Westleton, although – containing more poor heathland within their boundaries – they had rather lower population densities. Other parishes fall, in a pleasantly predictable manner, midway between the two extremes of 'open' and 'closed', such as Frostenden, divided between three main owners and with a moderately dense population, several shops, but no chapels or public houses.

Yet several local settlements clearly go against the model. Aldringham, for example, was owned in its entirety by Alexander Ogilvie in the 1880s and its population was low (524 people in a parish of 1,873 acres); but there was nevertheless a Baptist chapel here, and another in the hamlet of Thorpe (White 1885, 96). Wangford was a densely-settled village, with 606 people on 851 acres, numerous shops and a Primitive Methodist chapel, but the parish was almost wholly owned by the Earl of Stradbroke, who lived at nearby Henham (Glyde 1856, 326). Personal preferences and estate policy, and whether the 'closed'

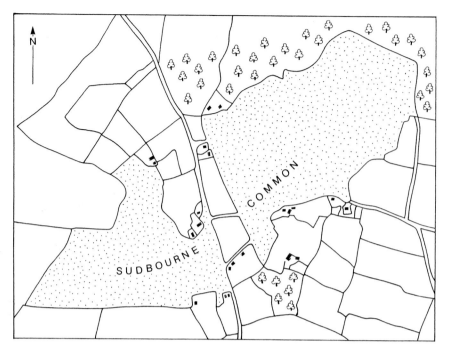

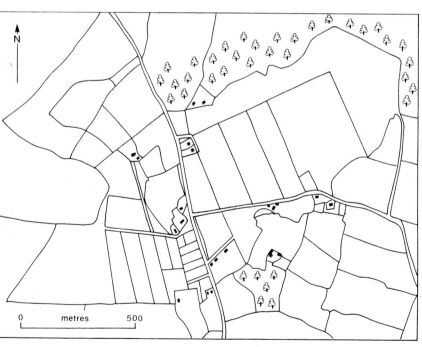

FIGURE 35.
left and opposite
The development of
Sudbourne village.
Before 1807, there was
no nucleated settlement
here but only a large
common, with a loose
scatter of dwellings
around its periphery
(top left). The common
was enclosed and
divided in 1807,
following parliamentary
enclosure (below left),
and by 1905 a small
nucleated settlement
had developed here
(top right). This has
since developed into a
substantial village
(below right).

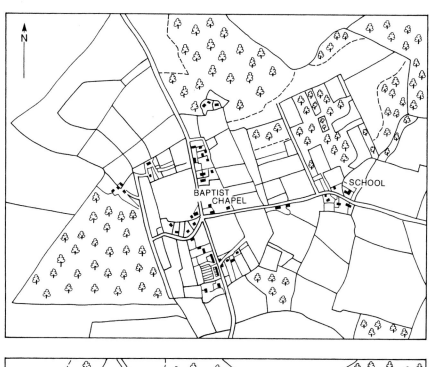

village was the actual residence of the landowner, evidently served to disrupt the neat models of the historical geographers. More importantly, it is likely that some of the parishes which fit the model, especially on the poorest soils in the south of the district, do so for reasons which are more complex than it assumes. Places like Gedgrave, Chillesford, Wantisden or Hazelwood, which in the later nineteenth century completely lacked shops, chapels or public houses, and which in 1881 had population densities ranging from 27 to as low as 9 per square kilometre, were owned by single individuals. They were the property of absentee owners, living many miles away, or else formed peripheral, outlying parts of Sandlings estates. Yet to a large extent it was probably the poverty of the soil which encouraged both low population densities (and the consequent lack of shops and other facilities) *and* single ownership: it was relatively easy for individuals to acquire such places *in toto*, for the price of this poor land was so low. Today, these are all still tiny places, a small cluster of houses in the case of Chillesford, a thin scatter of farms and cottages in the case of the others. Hazelwood church was already in ruins at the start of the nineteenth century, and has now disappeared; that at Gedgrave had disappeared before this date (Kirby 1829, 153–4).

Parishes and hundreds

Medieval and post-medieval settlements, and their inhabitants, existed within a mesh of boundaries, some clearly marked and obvious, others known but invisible. Some defined the strips of individual farmers, or the units of rotation – the furlongs and fields – which they cultivated. Others bounded units of justice, taxation or administration. Of the latter, two are of particular interest to historians, and are usually traceable on relatively recent maps: those of the parish, the territory attached to and which supported a parish church; and those of the hundred, a unit of medieval administration, taxation and law enforcement.

Four main hundreds had land which largely or entirely fell within the area of the Sandlings: from north to south, Blything, Plomesgate, Wilford and Colneis, with Samford comprising the Shotley peninsula (Martin 1999d). The district also included small parts of Carlford and Mutford hundreds, and detached fragments of Loes and Hoxne. The hundred was established in the late Saxon period as a unit intermediate between the vill and the shire, but many examples were probably created in part out of much older territories, dating back to middle Saxon times or even beyond. Their boundaries were often chopped and changed over time to meet the convenience of administrators but are, nevertheless, often self-evidently ancient. They thus frequently follow important topographic features, such as major watercourses or watersheds, while hundreds themselves can correspond to major drainage systems. Peter Warner has suggested that Blything Hundred is one with an ancient history, a unit which may have had the status of a tribal territory in early Saxon times, later developing into a petty kingdom and ultimately into a major royal estate (Warner 1996, 156–9). Its area corresponded, more or less, with the drainage basin of the river Blyth and its name means simply 'the people of the river Blyth'. The royal vill and ancient ecclesiastical site ('minster') of Blythburgh, 'the fort on the Blyth', lay at its centre, and nearby Dunwich may originally have been the *wic*, or trading place, of its early Saxon rulers (Haslam 1992). To the south the hundreds of Loes, Wilford and Plomesgate, which were interdigitated in complex ways, together probably formed another ancient territory, separated by the Deben estuary from a third, comprising the hundreds of Colneis and Carlford. These five hundreds were later combined into a unit called Wicklaw, a Liberty (an area where royal jurisdiction was delegated) granted in 970 to the Abbey of Ely, but their configuration suggests that they originally formed two distinct territories. Close to the centre of the Loes/Wilford/Plomesgate territory lies Rendlesham, the ancient palace mentioned by Bede, and this block of land was thus presumably the heartland of the Wuffingas. Early tribal elites seem to have buried their dead on the boundaries of their lands, and it is noteworthy that the great burial ground of Sutton Hoo overlooks the Deben, the southern boundary of this putative territory. In a similar way, the cemetery at Snape lies close to the southern boundary of Blything hundred, although it admittedly lies at an inconvenient distance from Blythburgh itself.

Parish boundaries are probably, for the most part, less ancient than those of hundreds. Parishes developed in the course of the later Saxon period as local lords or groups of freemen erected churches within the much larger territories (or *parochiae*) of minsters – the 'mother churches' from which, in the early days of Christianity, groups of priests had served the spiritual needs of the local population (Blair 1988). For this reason the boundaries of parishes often preserve those of earlier estates and vills, although in detail their course was often defined only at a relatively late stage – especially where they crossed areas of open heath. Parochial patterns are intricate and instructive. As already noted, not every Saxon settlement in the Sandlings was a vill, and not every vill became a parish. Anomalies in the layout of boundaries can suggest where ancient territorial units, or the lands of lost settlements, have been absorbed. Thus Staverton, which was a substantial vill and manor at the time of Domesday, no longer exists as a settlement but only as the name of the ancient wood-pasture of Staverton Park. Its territory was presumably divided between the parishes of Eyke (where Staverton Hall is recorded on Norden's survey of 1600–01, close to what is now Friday Street) and Wantisden, and its disappearance almost certainly explains the curious extension of the latter parish to the south of the Butley river, embracing much of Staverton Park. The northern extension of Hollesley parish a short distance away may similarly mark the territory of an ancient settlement based on Manor Farm, perhaps the lost Domesday vill of *Laneburh*.

Even when early vills became parishes, they often lost that status in late medieval or early-modern times. On these poor soils farmers often found it hard to make a living, especially in times of recession, and some small settlements declined to the status of hamlets or individual farms incapable of maintaining a church which had been erected and embellished with the pious enthusiasm of earlier generations, larger or wealthier in character. The parish of Thorpe was thus eventually combined with its neighbour Aldringham, and Sizewell with Leiston: the names of the modern parishes (Aldringham with Thorpe, Leiston with Sizewell) signal this clearly. Elsewhere the configuration of parish boundaries once again gives the game away. The tiny vill of Dunningworth, on the southern bank of the Alde, achieved parochial status some time in the twelfth or thirteenth century but gradually declined thereafter, the *Suffolk Traveller* reporting in 1829 that:

> The church was standing and in use in the year 1561; but seems to have fallen into decay soon after; and has been so long down that there are no ruins of it left; so that this place is now considered as a hamlet of Tunstall (Kirby 1829, 152).

The land of Dunningworth is clearly apparent on modern maps as a bulging northern extension of Tunstall parish.

Open field and enclosure

The earliest surviving maps of Sandlings parishes, dating from the early seventeenth century, show a landscape in which hedged closes were interspersed with 'open fields' – that is, areas of arable in which the holdings of farmers took the form of intermingled unhedged strips, each generally less than half an acre in extent (Figures 36 and 37). The documentary sources suggest that in medieval times most arable land in the district lay in such fields, references to which outnumber those to enclosed land. Some time between 1157 and 1174, for example, William de Chesney granted to Blythburgh Priory 'twenty acres in *Westfield*' in Blythburgh (Harper-Bill 1980, no. 42); while in the late thirteenth century John son of Roger Coleman of Wenhaston granted the monks eight acres and one small piece of land (*pictellum*) lying 'in the field of Blythburgh' (Harper-Bill 1980, no. 53). In the early thirteenth century the Blythburgh Priory charters record a grant of two parcels of arable land (*duas pecias terre arabilis*) in Bulcamp, one of which lay 'between the land which was of William of Kerdiston and the land which was Simon the brother of John Band, of which one end abuts on the king's highway towards the west and the other end abuts above the land of William Fuc towards the east' (Harper Bill 1980, no. 89). Thirteenth-century grants of land in Holton refer to 'the field which is called Langemoor', 'the field which is called Medwe' and 'the field which is called Subbiscroft' (Harper Bill 1981, no. 323). The strips within the open fields were not entirely unbounded; most seem to have been separated from their neighbours by narrow unploughed grass balks. At Ufford in the eighteenth century fifty-three acres of open arable, divided into seventy-four strips, were said to be 'so intermixed with other lands that they could not be set out, the balks having been ploughed up'

Willm Myles

Ielsope

L

E

Alexander
Smythe

D

N

Antony
Ielsope

L

Antony Ielsope
M Edy wood

Antony

Ielsope

K

Antony
Ielsope

S

Anvill

Iohn olborne

B

Aylmers

C

Iohn
Olburne

A

Io: Olborne

A

A

Iohn

A

Turmill comon feylde

Olborne C

Peter
olburne

TV

Io. Olburnes

E

Iohn Olburne

D

Thomas
Cookes

Iohn olborne

F

Robe
Brigh

I

Thom
Cook

87

The Howes

Howhills

Common Heath of the
Manor of Sutton Hall

Sutton
All
Saints

Sandgreen

Woodhall

Pisterhall

Brickiln
Wood

Bedington's
Wood

0   1 km

N

(Burrell 1960, 44). Some areas of enclosed land, reclaimed directly from commons and heaths, always existed in the district, and there were also some small enclosed fields subdivided into strips, quite separate from the normal open fields. But for the most part open fields, subject to some measure of communal organisation, seem to have dominated the medieval Sandlings landscape.

In the Midland counties of England, where open-field agriculture reached its most developed form, the lands of each farmer were usually scattered, fairly evenly, through two or three great unhedged fields, one of which lay 'fallow', or uncropped, each year. The Sandlings, however, seems to have had a more 'irregular' system of open-field agriculture (Postgate 1973, 292–3, 299–300; Burrell 1960, 23–36). The settlement pattern was more dispersed than in the Midlands, as we have seen, and holdings were generally clustered in the vicinity of particular farms rather than being scattered widely through the territory of the village (Burrell 1960, 33). Cropping arrangements were usually less rigidly controlled by the community and, instead of lying in a single great 'field', the uncropped or 'fallow' land was usually scattered in discontinuous furlongs.

By the end of the sixteenth century, in most parishes, open fields were already disappearing through piecemeal enclosure – a process rather different from the large-scale, planned or 'general' enclosure which usually removed the more 'regular' open fields of the Midland counties (Farrand 2002). Piecemeal enclosure involved a series of private agreements which led to the amalgamation, through purchase and exchange, of groups of contiguous open-field strips, and their subsequent fencing or hedging, so that islands of enclosed land appeared within the fields. Sometimes enclosure proceeded in such a way that individual strips remained within a larger enclosed block which was otherwise in single ownership. In particular, strips of glebe land often survived in this way within someone else's property. Incumbents were, in effect, trustees rather than freehold owners and could not exchange land as easily as their neighbours. A survey of Walton-cum-Trimley made in 1613 describes 'one close of arable called Neweclose latelie taken out of Longhand Field late divers persons wherein John Talbot hath a single peece, containing 1 rod, 30 perches and the Vicar of Walton hath a single peece of Glebe land there containing 1 rod, 10 perches, the residue being Bull's containing 4 acres, 3 rods, 17 perches' (IRO HB 8: 1/202). The process of enclosure was a gradual one, the precise chronology of which varied considerably from parish to parish. In some places extensive areas of open field still existed at the start of the seventeenth century, as at Felixstowe in 1613, where there were four fields – South Field, North Field, Church Field and Myll Field (IRO HB: 8/1/202). At Walton, in contrast, there was much more enclosed land although the same survey nevertheless lists over 200 small strips, located in blocks of widely varying size and interspersed with the enclosed land (IRO HB: 8/1/202). But in some parishes, such as Rendlesham, Bromeswell, Tunstall and Orford, surveyed by John Norden in 1600–01, relatively little

FIGURE 37.
Map of the parish of Sutton, surveyed in 1631 by William Haiward, showing a mixture of open fields and hedged closes, most of the latter evidently enclosed piecemeal from the former (after Peter Warner).

open arable remained by this time, and the landscape was dominated by hedged closes (IRO V5/22/1EE5/11/1).

Maps and documents from the seventeenth and eighteenth centuries describe the continuing process of enclosure (Farrand 2002). In Reydon, for example, a seventeenth-century survey noted how one tenant held 'six acres of land neither more nor less ... in six pieces lately enclosed in one close' (IRO HA 11/C2/10). In 1679 in the same parish another tenant was said to hold 'one newly made enclosure, formerly several pieces' (IRO HA 11/C2/10). Court rolls sometimes record the process of exchange which preceded enclosure, as at Walton in 1606, where William Scruton exchanged various pieces of land with Richard Martin (IRO HA 119.50: 3/37–40). But piecemeal enclosure did not always, or even usually, involve the amicable swapping of strips between different proprietors. It was often associated with *engrossment* – that is, with the steady build-up of large estates at the expense of small owners. The court rolls of the manor of Westleton thus show how the holding of Edward Bedingfield grew, in the thirty years between 1569 and 1598, from 72 to 225 acres. Bedingfield's heir, Anthony, purchased an additional 60 acres in 1598–99 (WSRO 137/1/88). Often, however, compact blocks of land seem to have developed through a combination of both exchange and purchase. At Snape in the early seventeenth century the whole of the North Field – formerly twenty separate strips – was acquired by a single individual through a complex process of purchase and exchange (Burrell 1960, 122).

In many parishes open arable had been completely extinguished by the start of the eighteenth century, but in others the process of enclosure was more extended, as at Ufford, where forty-four acres divided into fifteen strips still existed when the Tithe Award map was surveyed in 1844. Occasionally, such residual areas were finally removed by parliamentary enclosure, by acts which were primarily concerned with the division and allotment of open commons. That for Bucklesham and Foxhall, for example, while specifically described as 'An Act for dividing, allotting, and inclosing heaths plains commons and waste ground' in the two parishes, also made provision for the exchange and consolidation of thirty pieces of arable land, totalling around seventy-five acres and ranging in size from a single rood to nine acres (IRO 150/1/3.15).

Piecemeal enclosure, because it involved the gradual hedging or fencing along the margins of groups of strips, tended to preserve in simplified form the essential layout of the old open landscape. Open-field plough strips seldom had dead straight boundaries. They were usually slightly curving or sinuous in plan, sometimes taking the form of a shallow 'reversed S', caused by the way that the ploughman moved to the left with his team as he approached the headland at the end of the strip, in order to avoid too tight a turning circle (Eyre 1955). Because the new hedges were established along the edges of bundles of strips, they served to preserve, in simplified form, these slightly wavy lines of the earlier landscape. In addition, because open-field strips running end to end seldom came to be enclosed at the same time by this

method, field patterns produced by piecemeal enclosure often exhibit numerous small 'kinks', tiny dog-legs, where the boundary of one field runs, not to the corner of the next field, but to a point some way along the boundary line, a strip or two strip's distance away (Figure 38).

Field patterns like this are ubiquitous on seventeenth-century maps of the district, but they are much less common in the modern landscape, which is instead dominated by carefully surveyed, ruler-straight boundaries (Figure 39). Many of the latter are to be found in areas of former heathland, and were evidently laid out in the seventeenth, eighteenth and nineteenth centuries as private sheep walks were subdivided and ploughed. Others result from the parliamentary enclosure of common heaths, as at Reydon, where the enclosure act of 1798 created straight-sided fields out of 504 acres of

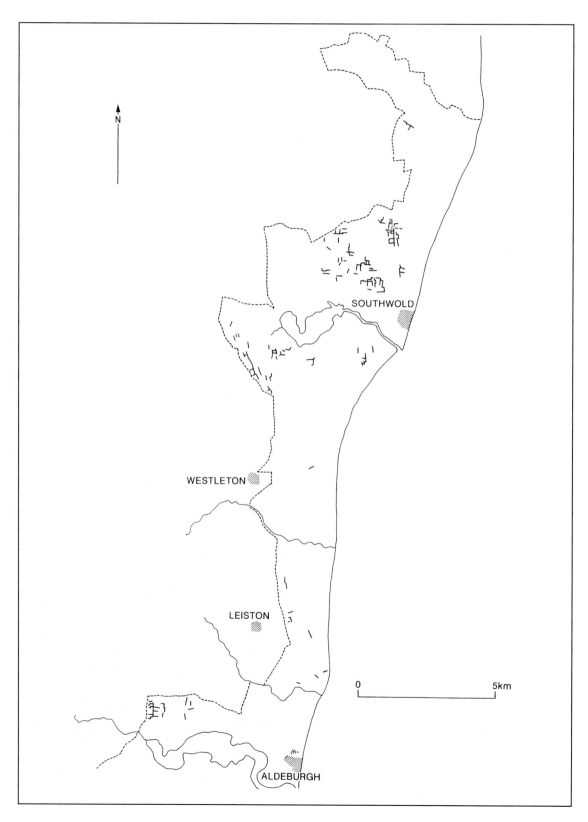

SOUTHWOLD

WESTLETON

LEISTON

0   5km

ALDEBURGH

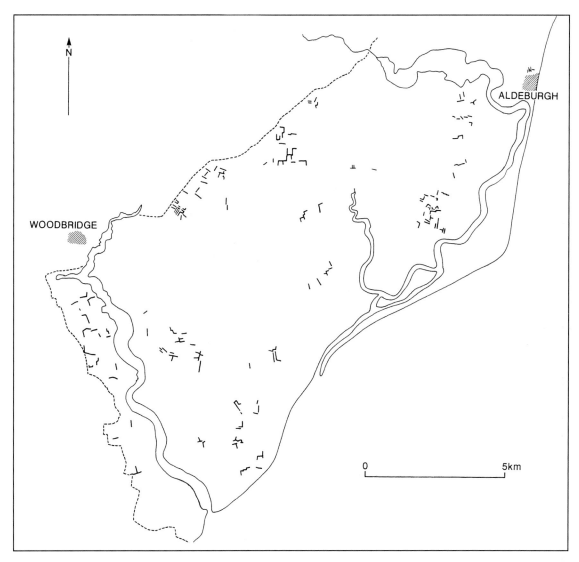

N

WOODBRIDGE

ALDEBURGH

0   5km

FIGURE 39.
opposite and above
The distribution of
field boundaries created
through piecemeal
enclosure in the
Sandlings in *c.* 1905. By
this time, they
constituted only a small
minority of boundaries
in the district.

common land, mainly heath, which were divided between the principal owners; the remaining 2,090 acres of the parish already lay in hedged fields, most of it former open-field arable which had been enclosed piecemeal (IRO B/50/1/2). Yet rectilinear field patterns predominate almost everywhere – even within areas which early maps show were divided into fields displaying the sinuous, irregular boundaries resulting from the piecemeal enclosure of open fields, or direct enclosure from the wastes. Evidently, as more and more land fell into the hands of large estates in the course of the eighteenth and nineteenth centuries, existing field patterns were comprehensively redrawn, just as the district's settlement pattern was extensively re-organised. Old boundaries were straightened or removed and new ones laid out, in order to create the 'rational' patterns demanded by landowners and their tenants in this age of improvement.

Hedges

The majority of field boundaries in the Sandlings are defined by hedges, in varying states of preservation and under various forms of management. As in other areas of East Anglia, large numbers were removed in the course of the twentieth century, most notably, perhaps, in the north of Sudbourne parish and to the south of Tunstall. But the mania for grubbing out hedges did not affect the Sandlings quite as much as it did the area of clay soils to the west, and many of the large prairie-like areas which can be found – as around Sutton – are not in fact the consequence of modern hedge removal, but are places where extensive areas of open heathland survived into the twentieth century, and were then ploughed.

It is sometimes suggested that we can learn much about the age and origins of hedgerows from studying their botanical composition. In the 1960s the ecologist Max Hooper suggested that, in broad terms, the number of different shrub species found in a standard thirty-metre length of hedge was equivalent to its age in centuries. A five-species hedge would thus be around five hundred years old (the method excludes climbers like brambles and honeysuckle) (Pollard, Hooper and Moore 1974, 79–85). The principal explanation for this observed relationship was that hedges acquire new species over time, but gradually, and at a roughly constant rate. The 'Hooper Hypothesis' was enthusiastically embraced by local historians and others in the 1970s and 80s, but more recent work has questioned its validity. Many early hedges were probably planted with a wide range of species (Johnson 1980) while variations in soils and seed supply seem to have had a major effect on rates of colonisation (Barnes and Williamson *in press* 2006; Williamson 2002, 77–85; Willmott 1980).

An examination of the hedges in the Sandlings district clearly demonstrates the limitations of the 'Hooper Hypothesis'. Throughout the district they are, in comparison with those found on the clay soils to the west, fairly species-poor, even those which seem to be of medieval or early post-medieval date – growing on roadsides and parish boundaries, or around apparent intakes from the waste or piecemeal enclosures from the open fields. Few boast more than four or five species per thirty-metre stretch: in the claylands, in contrast, not many hedges contain as few species as this. Hawthorn and sloe are well-represented, with some oak, gean (wild cherry), hazel, ash, dogrose, elder and elm, and the occasional maple, but few other species are present in any numbers. Almost certainly, this comparative botanical poverty is a consequence of environmental factors: the district's acid soils and, perhaps, proximity to the coast. Moreover, many of these early hedges are dominated by, and a large number almost entirely composed of, elm (Figure 40). Some examples may have been planted with this species but in most cases it seems to be invasive, suckering vigorously from long-felled hedgerow trees. On poor, leached soils elm can quite rapidly out-compete other hedgerow species, and it does particularly well in coastal areas, being more resistant to the effects

FIGURE 40.
Elm hedge in
Covehithe: hedges
composed mainly or
entirely of elm are a
characteristic feature of
the Sandlings
landscape.

of salt than other shrubs. Although some straight hedges of eighteenth- and nineteenth-century date are also dominated by elm, the majority are composed of hawthorn or (more rarely) sloe, accompanied by small amounts of rose, elder, elm and ash, although on the poorest soils (and in the most exposed coastal locations) many consist almost entirely of sloe and hawthorn.

Most field boundaries in the Sandlings thus consist of mixed but relatively species-poor hedges; hedges dominated by elm; or hedges largely composed of either hawthorn or sloe. But not all the district's fields are bounded by hedges. In the area around Alderton and Ramsholt, and between Wantisden and Chillesford, some are surrounded by narrow belts of conifers – usually Scots pine (*Pinus sylvestris)*, occasionally Corsican pine (*Pinus nigra*). These appear to be of nineteenth- or even twentieth-century date: most are not shown on the Tithe Award maps of *c.* 1840, appearing for the first time on the Ordnance Survey First Edition six inch maps of *c.* 1890; some are more recent still. In addition, a small number of fields are bounded by lines of individual Scots pine trees, a feature of the landscape more usually associated with the

Breckland of north-western Suffolk. There are good examples in the area immediately to the south of Butley and, widely scattered, in the triangle formed by Alderton, Hollesley, and Sutton. Some of the trees have a slightly twisted form indicating that they were originally managed as low hedges (Figure 41). As in Breckland, pines were presumably selected for their ability to thrive on the poor sandy soils, and to rapidly provide shelter for crops and game, as well as some protection against the erosion to which these light sandy soils are prone. Most of the pine rows appear, once again, to be relatively recent additions to the landscape (Williamson 2002, 87–8).

A very small number of hedges in the district are composed largely of lilac, especially in the area around Alderton and Trimley; a fine example borders the road leading north from Alderton (TM344428). Most are found in the immediate area of settlements, although individual lilac bushes, or short sections of lilac, occur more widely. The plant seems to have spread into hedges from local gardens, its successful diffusion doubtless a consequence of its ability to thrive on poor acid soils and out-compete native hedging plants. It is also a fairly common component of Breckland hedges. Hedges containing the Duke of Argyll's Tea Plant (*Lycium barburum*), a plant introduced into Britain from Asia in the eighteenth century, are also occasionally found, again mainly in the south of the district, especially around Bawdsey, with one or two scattered examples – as at Erwarton – on the Shotley peninsula (Land Use Consultants 1999). In this case, the presence and occasional dominance of the species is probably a consequence not of natural colonisation, but of intentional planting. A small number of hedges were actually created from scratch using this species, apparently in the nineteenth century, but in other instances the plant is evidently a later addition, planted to fill up gaps. Lastly, hedges containing substantial quantities of holly, and (more occasionally) hedges containing very little else, are a notable feature of the extreme south of the district – the area of the Shotley peninsula, outside the Sandlings *sensu stricto*. They are especially prominent in the Woolverstone area. The most striking examples occur close to Woolverstone Park and home farm and are presumably a consequence of the planting policies of past owners or estate managers.

Seventeenth- and eighteenth-century maps of Sandlings estates show that the local hedges were thickly studded with trees, but today most are only sparsely-timbered. Large numbers of elms grew here before the appearance of Dutch Elm disease in the 1970s, and their loss had a very significant impact on the local landscape. But oaks were also well represented in Sandlings hedges, and even beech trees were occasionally noted by nineteenth-century writers. In the period before the late eighteenth century the majority of hedgerow trees were *pollarded* – that is, repeatedly cut at a height of around two metres in order to produce a regular crop of straight 'poles' suitable for fuel, fencing, buildings repairs etc. After this date, the numbers of pollards seems to have been reduced – great estates had a particular antipathy to this form of management. Nevertheless, as late as 1901 the 'picturesque pollard oaks and beeches, which flourish here in great luxuriance' were noted as a feature of the Sudbourne estate (*Country Life* 1901, 240) and examples of the former can still be found in the older hedges, especially along roadsides, as on the lanes to the east of Westleton and to the west of Covehithe (Figure 42).

Buildings in the landscape

Visitors probably notice a region's buildings more than any other aspect of its landscape. However, the architectural heritage of the Sandlings is, perhaps, one of its less striking aspects. Certainly, the district is not characterised by an abundance of fine medieval timber-framed houses, in sharp contrast to the clayland districts lying to the west, where substantial numbers of fourteenth- and fifteenth-century houses, and even a scatter dating from the thirteenth century, can be found (Coleman 1999; Coleman and Barnard 1999). The reasons for this paucity are uncertain but are presumably connected with the Sandling's relative poverty in the late medieval centuries, although it is surprising that more early buildings have not so far been discovered in major towns like Southwold or Aldeburgh, in spite of the serious fires which these places have suffered through the centuries. In nearby Woodbridge, certainly, fashionable eighteenth-century facades hide a number of fifteenth- and early sixteenth-century houses.

The only medieval buildings to make a significant impact on the Sandlings landscape are thus its parish churches. Most are constructed of flint, transported from the boulder clay areas to the west or collected from local beaches, but with corners and openings made of limestone brought from Northamptonshire or northern France. The local Coraline Crag has been used in a few places – for the towers of Wantisden and Chillesford churches, for example – while the smooth grey or brown limestone/clay nodules called 'septaria', which occur in the London clay in the south of the region, were also occasionally employed. Parish churches form a particularly striking feature of the local landscape because of the relatively level terrain, and because they stand, in many cases, outside or on the margins of settlements. Some – especially in the smaller parishes – are complex multi-period structures, often incorporating features of twelfth-century date, as at Butley, Middleton, South Cove, Sudbourne, Wantisden or Theberton – the latter with a Norman round tower, a feature which also appears as far south as Ramsholt and which displays the district's affinity, in cultural terms, with Norfolk and north-east Suffolk, rather than with south-west Suffolk. The most striking churches in the district, however – and, arguably, the most iconic – are the large, wealthy, late medieval structures found at places like Southwold, Blythburgh or Covehithe, built largely or entirely in the Perpendicular style and featuring lavish displays of knapped flintwork, and flushwork – that is, freestone decoration infilled with knapped flints. Southwold, 43 metres long and with a tower 30 metres high, dominates the landscape far and wide; Blythburgh, 38 metres long and with a tower 25

FIGURE 41.
opposite above
Pine row near Butley
church: the pines'
twisted growth pattern
suggests that they were
originally plashed, to
form a hedge.

FIGURE 42.
opposite below
Old pollarded oak tree
in a roadside hedge
near Covehithe.

FIGURE 43.
Blythburgh church, one
of several substantial
late medieval churches
in the Sandlings,
occupies a
commanding position
overlooking the Blyth
Creek.

metres high, is even more impressive, as it stands on rising ground above the mudflats and reedbeds beside the river Blyth (Figure 43). Many of these great buildings were constructed from scratch, not as modifications of existing edifices, although earlier masonry was often freely reused, as at Blythburgh, where Norman window-heads can be traced in the external faces of the walls. Some were too large for later communities to maintain. Covehithe and Walberswick are both dramatic examples of later retrenchment, with small, functioning churches now standing within the ruins of much larger late medieval buildings. At Covehithe, the church fell into ruins during the Civil War and the diminutive brick and thatched structure which stands within its shell was put up in 1672 (Pevsner 1974, 159). At Walberswick nearly three-quarters of the church were demolished in 1697. Travel writers and antiquaries have often seen these truncated structures as evidence for a local decline in the size of local settlements and populations, perhaps caused by coastal erosion (especially in the case of Covehithe). But the scale of parish churches, especially in late medieval times, did not closely reflect the size of the communities which they served, but rather the wealth of particular families, who donated money for additions or alterations in the hope of a speedy passage through purgatory for themselves or loved ones. The great perpendicular churches of the district, especially the great chain from Kessingland

through Covehithe, Southwold, Blythburgh and Walberswick to Aldeburgh, testify above all to commercial wealth, derived from the sea.

Most of the local monastic houses were treated as quarries after the Reformation. But there are important fragments of the thirteenth-century Franciscan friary at Dunwich, while at Leiston the house of the Premonstratensian canons – originally founded at Minsmere in 1182, moved to this site in 1363, and rebuilt following a fire in 1382 – there are more extensive remains (Mortimer 1979, 98). The ruins of the great church, originally 50 metres in length, survive, partly built into a more recent house. Together with much of the cloister and principal ranges (New 1985, 236–8) (Figure 44), it makes an impressive *ensemble* by East Anglian standards, which is now under the care of English Heritage. At Butley only a single arch remains of the Priory church, once one of the largest in East Anglia, and no trace remains of the claustral ranges (Dickens 1951, xi). But the magnificent gatehouse, built in the 1320s, still survives, converted into a house in the early eighteenth century. It is one of the most important fourteenth-century buildings in Suffolk and famous for its flamboyant display of flushwork decoration (Pevsner 1974, 137–40).

Secular high-status residences from the middle ages have left fewer traces. On the Sandlings proper there are no surviving examples of medieval manor houses and even moats are a rarity. They were difficult to construct on these porous soils and were unnecessary for drainage: only a handful of examples are known, on exposures of the underlying London Clay (as at Capel Hall in Trimley) or in areas of low-lying marsh (as at Alderton, where there is a double moat) (Martin 1999c). As for larger residences – the castles of major landowners – that at Walton (built within the ruins of a Roman 'Saxon Shore' fort) was destroyed by coastal erosion, as we have seen, and its site now lies more than 200 metres offshore, but that erected by Henry II at Orford between 1165 and 1173, at a total cost of £1413 9s 2d, is still immensely impressive (Allen, Potter and Poulter 2002, 39) (Figure 45). The curtain walls and towers, which were illustrated by John Norden in his survey of the Stanhope estates (IRO EE5/11/1), had disappeared by the start of the nineteenth century but the great keep remains, remarkably well-preserved, dominating the new town which Henry laid out beside it. It is constructed of septaria, together with limestone brought from Caen in northern France and Northamptonshire. Its plan – with a circular interior but polygonal exterior, and three projecting towers – is unique, and incorporates a chapel, a basement store room with a well, as well as a cistern, constructed within the thickness of the walls, to collect rainwater from the roof. It is often suggested that the castle formed part of a plan to curb the power of the Bigod family, who held nearby Walton castle and who led a rebellion against the king in 1173–74; but construction of Orford began as early as 1165, when relations between the young king and Hugh Bigod were still relatively friendly (Allen, Potter and Poulter 2002, 36–9). Its coastal location may imply a response to a foreign threat, perhaps an anticipated French invasion associated with the supporters of Thomas a

Becket. Either way, the precise location of castle and associated port was clearly decided by the excellent harbourage then offered by the mouth of the Ore, and perhaps by the fact that the area was relatively devoid of existing farms and settlements. Orford does not appear in Domesday Book, its area and resources being listed under neighbouring Sudbourne, and its church always remained a dependent chapel of that parish.

Examples of later sixteenth- and seventeenth-century vernacular houses are more numerous than those from earlier centuries, although once again they are not as common as on the claylands to the west. In relative terms, outside the main towns, the Sandlings remained poor in this period and, more importantly, much of its building stock was probably swept away in the course of the eighteenth and nineteenth centuries, especially in the south of the district, as great estates invested in extensive 'improvements'. Those pre-1700 houses which do survive follow the styles favoured elsewhere in northern and eastern Suffolk, with a preference for lobby entry types – in which the front door is in line with the chimney, and gives access to a small lobby against the stack. Most have their frames hidden by plasterwork, although examples of exposed framing are occasionally found. Many, moreover, were cased in red brick in the course of the eighteenth and nineteenth centuries, and it is brick buildings and facades of later seventeenth-, eighteenth- and nineteenth-century date which are the main characteristic of local villages, and of the small towns. These usually employ the soft red brick produced locally, set in grey mortar, but some grey, limed brick is also found, principally in the more upmarket nineteenth-century houses. Some cottages and small farms are thatched, but red or black pantiles are the characteristic roofing material of the district. These distinctive tiles have a section like a shallow 'S' and, unlike 'normal' plain tiles, they are not nailed or pegged into the roof battons, and are laid in such a way that each only overlaps one, rather than two, others. Pantiles were introduced into eastern England from the Low Countries – the Dutch word 'pan' means 'tile' – and were manufactured locally from the start of the eighteenth century (Brunskill 1978). They were often used to replace thatch. An innovation of the mid-eighteenth century was the glazed tile, usually black: glazing was mainly intended to protect the tile from frost cracking. Pantiles are a feature of the east coast of England, as far south as the Lark-Gipping corridor. Their distribution tends to fade out towards the south-west of Suffolk: once again, the Sandlings shows itself allied, in cultural terms, with northern East Anglia. Towards the south of the Sandlings proper, in coastal settlements like Orford, plain tiles are more prominent but it is only to the south of the river Orwell, on the Shotley peninsula, that they become dominant, and pantiles correspondingly rare.

The majority of post-medieval buildings are farmhouses and cottages but farm buildings – mainly of eighteenth- and nineteenth-century date and constructed of similar materials to the local houses – also make an important contribution to the landscape. Nonconformist chapels are thinly distributed, except in the major towns, for the reasons already discussed; while a scatter of

FIGURE 44.
Leiston Abbey: the
great church of the
best-preserved monastic
ruin in the Sandlings.

industrial buildings testifies, somewhat paradoxically, to the essentially *rural* nature of the local economy in the eighteenth and nineteenth centuries. The most notable of these is the huge maltings at Snape, built in a series of stages from the late 1840s by Newson Garrett (Simper 1967), one of the most impressive pieces of industrial archaeology in eastern England (Figure 46). The Houses of Industry at Tattingstone and at Bulcamp in Blythburgh are remarkably early examples of their type: that at Tattingstone was built in 1765 (and enlarged in 1819 and 1837), and that in Bulcamp in the same year, although it was partly destroyed soon afterwards in a riot and rebuilt. They are grim reminders of the widespread rural poverty and unemployment which underpinned the transformation of the local landscape in the course of the eighteenth and nineteenth centuries.

FIGURE 45.
Orford Castle, built by
Henry II in the 1160s,
is the most impressive
medieval building in
the Sandlings.

FIGURE 46.
The vast industrial
complex at Snape
Maltings, now
converted into a
concert hall, shops and
leisure facilities.

CHAPTER FIVE

Woods, Parks and Plantations

....

Introduction

The woodland which forms such an important component of the Sandlings landscape has diverse origins. While a few wooded areas date back to medieval times, far more numerous and extensive are those established by large estates during the eighteenth and nineteenth centuries – as a source of profit, to beautify the landscape and to provide cover for game. The largest areas by far, however, were created much more recently, during the first half of the twentieth century. These are the great conifer forests planted by the Forestry Commission which dominate, in particular, the landscape around Tunstall and Wantisden (Figure 47).

Medieval woodland

Ancient, semi-natural woods are numerous on the clay soils to the west but in the Sandlings themselves they are something of a rarity, and Domesday Book shows that there was already little woodland in the district (Rackham 1999). Nevertheless, there were more woods here in medieval times than the surviving examples might suggest. Edy Wood in Tunstall and Hubbards Grove in Dunningworth, for example, shown on Norden's 1601 survey of the Stanhope estates, had both disappeared by the early nineteenth century, perhaps falling victim to large landowners' fashionable antipathy to traditional woodland (IRO V5/22/1). Either way, only a handful of woods with ancient origins now survive in the district, and these often in degraded condition: Iken Wood, which was partially destroyed in the last century; Reydon Wood, largely replanted (Rackham 1986); the remains of Sudbourne Great Wood and Captain's Wood in Sudbourne; together with, probably, Woodhall Wood and Rockhall Wood in Sutton, both of which appear on a map of 1631. In addition, a number of woods on the Shotley peninsula appear to have medieval origins, including Freston Wood, although, again, all have been extensively replanted in comparatively recent times.

Medieval woods were intensively managed. In most, the majority of trees and shrubs were *coppiced*, cut down close to ground level every few years, in order to produce a regular crop of straight 'poles' suitable for firewood, fencing, and a host of other uses (Rackham 1976 and 1986). The timber trees, or *standards*, were comparatively few in number (in order to avoid shading out the coppice stools). Such woods were usually enclosed with substantial banks and fences or hedges, in order to protect the regenerating coppice stools from browsing livestock. The surviving remains of the Sandlings examples suggest that the timber trees were mainly oaks, while the understorey was composed principally of hazel, birch, holly and rowan (Beardall and Casey 1995, 86–7).

There was, however, another way in which wood and timber were produced in the Middle Ages. 'Wood-pastures' were areas in which livestock were grazed as well as trees grown. The majority of the trees were pollarded, regularly cut for poles in the same way as coppices but at a height of around two metres, out of reach of the animals. Some wood pastures were common land but many were private, most notably the parks of the gentry and aristocracy, in which deer were grazed beneath the trees (Rackham 1986, 122–9; Hoppitt 1992).

The Sandlings boasts one of the most important surviving areas of wood pasture in England – Staverton Park. It consists of *c.* 200 acres (*c.* 81 hectares)

FIGURE 47.
below and overleaf
The extensive woodlands of the Sandlings are of varying origins, but the overwhelming majority were planted in the period after *c.* 1750.

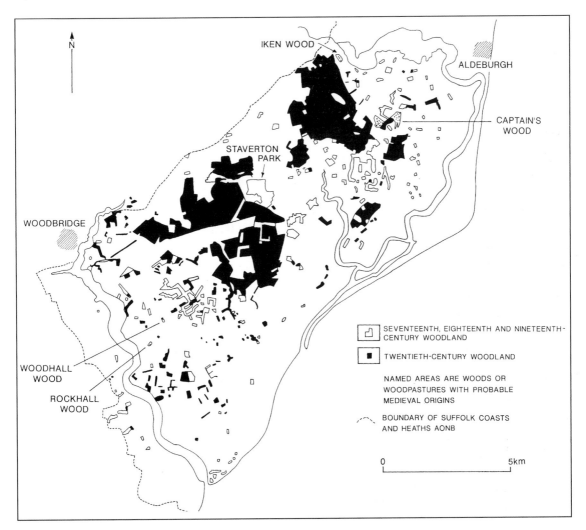

SEVENTEENTH, EIGHTEENTH AND NINETEENTH-CENTURY WOODLAND

TWENTIETH-CENTURY WOODLAND

NAMED AREAS ARE WOODS OR WOODPASTURES WITH PROBABLE MEDIEVAL ORIGINS

BOUNDARY OF SUFFOLK COASTS AND HEATHS AONB

0   5km

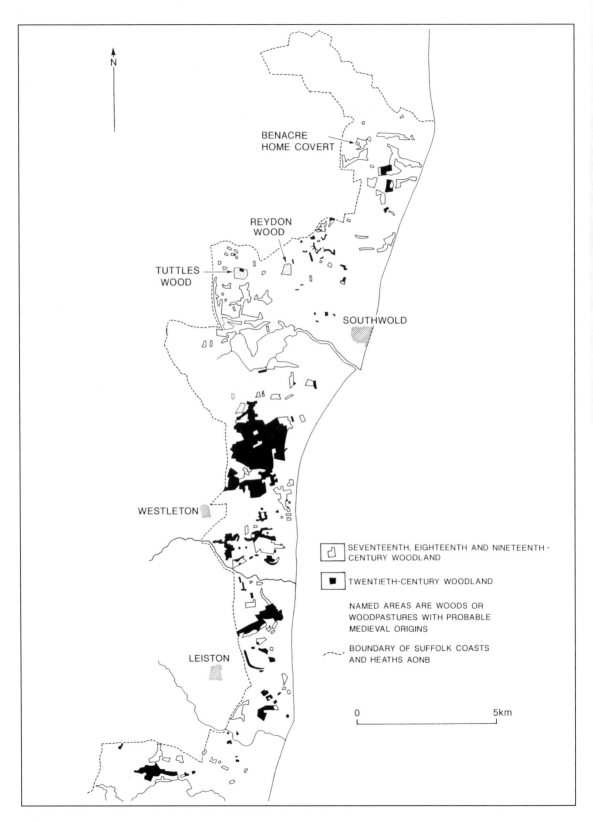

FIGURE 48.
Staverton Park, near
Wantisden, is one of
the finest surviving
medieval wood pastures
in England.

of close-set oak pollards, lying on the boundary between the parishes of Wantisden and Eyke. Soil profiles suggest that the area has never been fully cleared or brought under cultivation (Peterken 1968): it is a magical place (Figure 48). We first hear of the park in 1268 but it may have much earlier origins. There is no obvious reason why an extensive wood-pasture should have survived here, when the adjacent heathlands were stripped bare of trees, and its proximity to Rendlesham hints that it may have originated as a Saxon hunting ground. Either way, the park was owned by the Bigod family until 1306, when – on the death of Roger Bigod – it reverted to the Crown and was granted to the Earl of Norfolk. It remained the property of successive earls until 1529, when it was sold to Butley Priory for £240. Following the Dissolution it passed through a variety of lay hands but, surprisingly, retained its coherence and character (Hoppitt 1992, 171–96). Surviving accounts from the fourteenth century refer to the use of the park for grazing and pannage, and to the sale of bracken, wood and timber. It also contained a rabbit warren. In late medieval times it appears to have ceased to function as a deer farm, an *Inquisition Post Mortem* for 1322 describing it as 'without deer, now greatly broken down'. Patent Rolls for 1385 record the appointment of a warrener, but not a park-keeper (Hoppitt 1992).

The warren survived into the sixteenth century but deer did not return to the park, although it continued to be grazed, and to serve as a major source of wood and timber. Henry VIII's sister Mary visited in 1528 and dinner was eaten *sub Quercubus* – under the oaks – with 'fun and games'. In the late sixteenth century the park was acquired by the Stanhope estate and Norden's survey of 1601 shows relatively dense tree cover across much of the park, interspersed with some open areas (IRO V5/22/1). Accounts describe the maintenance of the perimeter pale, and refer to the felling of oak, poplar and alder, and to poles, 'cropewood' and faggots cut from the pollards (Hoppitt 1992, 174–6). By 1779, to judge from a map surveyed by Isaac Johnson, the pollards had increased in number and now accounted for around half the area of the park (IRO HD 11/475/W; Hoppitt 1992). The eastern side had now been fenced off and incorporated within the adjacent sheep-walk; the southern and western edges had been ploughed. There were other changes in the course of the eighteenth century, according to Peterken, who carried out a detailed examination of the surviving trees (Peterken 1968). Pollarding seems to have come to an end, and at the same time the intensity of grazing probably declined, leading to the development of a fairly dense shrub layer consisting of hawthorn, birch, rowan and – in particular – holly (Peterken 1968). Kirby, in 1764, referred to the 'vast' quantities of holly growing there (Kirby 1764, 25). Subsequent changes were, however, minimal. The Tithe Award maps (Eyke: IRO FDA 93/A1/1a; Wantisden: IRO FDA 272/A1/1b) and the Ordnance Survey First Edition six inch map of 1880 show the same basic disposition of features as Johnson's survey of 1779, although with the eastern edge now ploughed, and with heathland now occupying the southern and western portions. By this time, the park – since the seventeenth century the property of the Wantisden estate – was principally used as game cover. Today, deer have been reintroduced and the entire area is carefully managed. Oak remains the dominant tree in the central parts of the park. The south-eastern section – known as Staverton Thicks – has a greater density of tree cover, and a greater range of species, including large quantities of rowan and holly.

Staverton was already considered a remarkable place in the eighteenth century, when Kirby described the 'thousands of pollarded oaks' there (Kirby 1764, 25). But other wood-pastures certainly survived in the district into the post-medieval period, especially on the heavier soils on its western fringes. Immediately to the north of Benacre Hall, buried in a much later wood called Home Covert, is a small group of close-set pollards – eighteen oaks and one elm, still alive – which is the remains of a diminutive wood-pasture shown here on a map of 1580 (LRO 629/3/2). Some of the trees are evidently medieval, others may have been established as late as the seventeenth century.

Post-medieval woodland

Such survivals from the medieval landscape are of incalculable value, in both historical and ecological terms. But far more numerous in the Sandlings are plantations of post-medieval date. A number of these were established before *c.* 1700 and were managed on traditional lines, as coppice-with-standards.

They are thus technically classified by botanists as 'ancient' woods, although they are secondary, rather than primary, in character. Examples include Watling Wood on the northern edge of Sudbourne Park, described in 1601 as 'a new wood full of young sette' (IRO V5/22/1); Holly Grove in Benacre; and (probably) Whitmore Wood in Rendlesham (Figure 49). In these woods, as in the surviving remnants of medieval woodland, oak is the dominant standard tree but the understorey is more uniform in character than that of earlier woods, and usually dominated by hazel or sweet chestnut.

The scale of estate planting increased in the course of the eighteenth century and escalated considerably during the nineteenth. But while existing coppiced woods were often still managed on traditional lines the vast majority of these new areas of woodland were *plantations*, without a coppiced understorey (Thomas 2003). Trees were planted, thinned, and then either harvested as a crop or left to grow on as a feature in the landscape. Most of these relatively recent woods are distinguished by their names: many are described as 'Covert', 'Belt', 'Broom', or 'Plantation' or, if dignified by the more traditional 'Wood', often have names referring to individuals, such as Alexander Wood and Margaret Wood in Aldringham. They display a wide range of shapes and sizes, from small and relatively geometric, through attenuated belts, to large and irregular areas. Many were principally established as game cover (as the frequent name 'Covert' indicates), reflecting the increasing obsession with pheasant shooting in the course of the nineteenth century. The great estates of the area, especially Sudbourne, were noted for their game, and it was on the Sudbourne and Rendlesham estates that the French partridge was first introduced into England in the middle of the nineteenth century (Wentworth Day 1979, 651). But plantations were also intended to beautify the landscape and to provide shelter for crops when areas of heathland were being reclaimed, as well as being a financial investment, a source of income for their owners.

The role of the larger landowners in the creation of these eighteenth and nineteenth-century plantations is clear from the particularly large concentrations found close to the mansions at the hearts of their estates, in and around their landscape parks, at Benacre, Henham and Rendlesham. These core areas were planted up in the course of the eighteenth century but the majority of the more distant plantations were only established in the period after *c.* 1780. Many, indeed, seem to have been planted after the Tithe Award maps of *c.* 1840 were surveyed: some, such as Tangham Forest in Capel St Andrew, were only created at the very end of the nineteenth century.

Many post-medieval plantations were comprehensively replanted in the course of the twentieth century, usually with conifers. The original planting, where it survives, is dominated by oak, but with some ash and beech. Sometimes the young trees required were purchased from commercial nurseries, but more often they were grown on the estate itself. Estate accounts from Henham in 1829 record payments for gathering acorns and haws from the local woods and fields while at Sudbourne, as late as 1901, an area close to the gardens was used as a 'nursery for growing forest trees of all kinds, from

FIGURE 49.
Whitmoor Wood,
Rendlesham, may be of
medieval origins but is
probably of sixteenth-
or seventeenth-century
date. Coppices of hazel
grow beneath a canopy
of oak trees.

which the great area of woods and plantations is renewed and restocked' (Thomas 2003, 231; IRO HA11/C41/2; *Country Life* 1901, 6).

Although in theory the distinction between these new plantations and the 'traditional' woods managed as coppice-with-standards is clear enough, in estate accounts it is rather less apparent (Thomas 2003, 220–48). Eighteenth- and nineteenth-century plantations were planted much more densely than those of today, partly because their owners were expecting serious losses (especially from rabbits) but also because foresters had no way of controlling weed growth, other than by shading it out. The trees were thinned on a number of successive occasions, and the thinnings are somewhat confusingly referred to in estate documents as 'poles' – the same as the term employed for the produce of coppices. Indeed, they seem to have been used in a similar range of ways. Particularly detailed wood and timber accounts survive for Henham in the mid nineteenth century (IRO HA 11/C41/2–4; Thomas 2003, 220–48) and these show clearly the frequent and systematic nature of thinning. Two acres of Easey's Covert, for example, was cut in 1856, around five in 1857, and four in 1859; while two acres of Southwold Covert were cut in 1856, five acres in 1857, and six in 1859. In some cases, the character of the work is given in more detail. In the autumn of 1828, for example, contractors were paid £8 0s 7d for work in Sand Pit Covey, the accounts detailing:

	£	s	d
For felling 910 firs @ 6s per hundred	2	4	6
For tying of 20 ¼ hundred of wood @ 3s	3	0	9
To carrying out 830 trees @ 2s 6d	1	0	7½
To carrying out 20 ¼ of wood @ 1s 6d	1	10	4½
Cutting 4 score of double binded furze faggots @ 10s	0	3	4
To carry out binded furze faggots	1	0	

Evidently, a comprehensive thinning and 'cleaning' operation was being undertaken (IRO HA 11/C41/2). The firs were here evidently a nurse crop, although some pure conifer plantations were established in the nineteenth century. Late nineteenth-century topographic writers imply that pine woods were a characteristic feature of the district and the Ordnance Survey First Edition six inch maps from the same period represent many areas of woodland as coniferous.

Modern plantations

The largest areas of woodland in the Sandlings comprise conifer plantations established by the Forestry Commission in the first half of the twentieth century (Figure 50). The Commission was created in 1921 as a consequence of the severe timber shortages experienced by the nation during the First World War. Two kinds of marginal land were chosen for planting – heathland and upland moor – and afforestation was intended, in part, to relieve problems of rural unemployment at a time of acute agricultural recession. The largest areas of afforestation in East Anglia were in the Breckland of north-west Suffolk and south-west Norfolk. The Sandlings forests were always less extensive and, while their history parallels in many ways that of the Breckland plantations, there are a number of differences in detail. Because of their comparative modernity, Forestry Commission plantations are usually ignored in studies of landscape history. But they make an important contribution to the appearance of the countryside, and now that they have been in existence, in many cases, for three-quarters of a century or more, they have themselves become a part of the historic landscape, as well as playing an important role in nature conservation (Skipper and Williamson 1997).

There are three main areas of forest in the Sandlings: Rendlesham, Tunstall and Dunwich, the latter always the smallest of the three. The story of Rendlesham Forest began in 1920 with the purchase of 1,878 acres (760 hectares) from Lord Rendlesham (Forestry Commission archives, Santon Downham: Acquisition Files, uncatalogued). This was followed by the acquisition of 699 acres (283 hectares), part of the Sutton Hoo estate, in 1926; and by further purchases from the Rendlesham estate – including the 1,144-acre (463-hectare) Rookery Farm in Rendlesham in 1925 and Red House and Walnut Tree farms, totalling 942 acres (381 hectares), in 1929. After this, purchases in the area tended to be on a smaller scale, generally of less than 40 hectares, and usually comprised areas of existing estate woodland, such as Culpho Wood and Ufford Thicks. These were, for the most part, rapidly replanted (Forestry Commission archives, Santon Downham: Acquisition Files, uncatalogued).

Tunstall Forest was built up more gradually. The Commission's first purchase was of 437 acres (177 hectares) from the Sudbourne estate in 1920, but no further land was bought until 1929, when 906 acres (367 hectares) of the Campsea Ashe estate was acquired, followed in 1930 by 1,600 acres (648 hectares) of the

Chillesford estate. In 1931 the 431 acres (174 hectares) of Walk Farm in Tunstall were acquired, and in the following year 133 acres (54 hectares) of Church Farm, Sudbourne, were bought. These acquisitions were followed in 1938 by the purchase of a further 185 acres (75 hectares) from the Campsea Ashe estate. Once again, after this only relatively small portions of land were added. In the 1920s and 30s the two areas – Rendlesham and Tunstall – were managed as a single unit, called Rendlesham Forest (Forestry Commission archives, Santon Downham: Acquisition Files, uncatalogued). By 1926 2,302 acres (932 hectares) had been planted, rising to 3,501 acres (1,417 hectares) by 1930. This was a remarkable achievement, given that the planting was done entirely by hand, after the heaths had been horse ploughed. By 1935 4,790 acres (1,938 hectares) had been afforested, reaching 4,905 acres (1,985 hectares) by 1938 (Butcher 1941, 331).

The much smaller Dunwich Forest began life rather later than the others, with the acquisition of 343 acres (139 hectares) from the Dunwich estate in 1925, followed by the purchase of 840 acres (340 hectares) from the Westleton estate in 1929 (Forestry Commission archives, Santon Downham: Acquisition Files, uncatalogued). By 1926, only 5 acres (*c.* 2 hectares) had been afforested, although this rose to 316 acres (128 hectares) by 1930 and 755 acres (305 hectares) by 1935. Afforestation thereafter remained at this relatively low level until a spate of post-Second World War purchases, again mainly of small blocks of land, most comprising less than 40 hectares.

Most of the land was bought cheaply, local land prices having plummeted during the course of the agricultural recession. The bulk was purchased for between £3 and £6 an acre. The vast majority comprised either heathland or derelict arable, the former tending to be more prominent in the earlier purchases. The Acquisition Reports often include important descriptions of the land's condition. When Walk Farm in Tunstall was bought in 1931, for example, the surveyor described how:

> Fine grasses with gorse and bracken are the principal features on the
> heath while the derelict arable fields carry the typical weeds of the locality
> and some bracken here and there … Only some 35 acres [out of 431] are
> now cultivated and the farm has for some time been kept in hand for the
> sake of the sporting (Forestry Commission archives, Santon Downham:
> acquisition files, uncatalogued)

Some poor arable land, still under cultivation, was also purchased. Much of this, following normal Forestry Commission policy, was used to provide small-holdings for forest workers, a sensible plan from the Commission's point of view as much forest work was seasonal in character:

> Forest holdings are designed to house the forest worker and give him a
> piece of land about ten acres to keep farm stock and to cultivate. He gets
> winter work in the forest for about 100 days and, for the rest of the year,
> he can devote himself to the cultivation of his holdings (Butcher 1941, 331)

As in Breckland, the Commission originally intended to plant a higher proportion of native hardwoods than was eventually the case. At Walk Farm, Tunstall, for example, Corsican Pine and Scots Pine were considered the principal potential crop in 1931, but the Acquisition Report noted that 'the possibilities of raising oak on part of the ground should be considered'. In 1938 at Tunstall, similarly, it was thought that 'portions of the area will carry oak and possibly ash can also be grown. A mixture of oak with Scots pine as the nurse species can be advocated, their mixture having been adopted in parts of the forest and found beneficial in the early stages of the establishment'. Few of the oaks or ashes that were planted thrived, however, falling victim to the droughty soils and, in particular, to the depredations of deer. Beech was more successful, but only ever amounted to a minority crop. The vast majority of the three forests thus came to be dominated by conifers – principally Corsican pine and Scots pine, with smaller areas of Douglas fir and European larch.

Objections to the spread of conifer plantations across the Sandlings heaths were being raised at least from the 1940s. At an informal meeting concerning recent and potential acquisitions of land by the Commission, held at the request of the Regional Controller of the Ministry of Town and Country Planning in 1949, the clerk of the East Suffolk County Council:

> Suggested that as the total suitable areas in East Suffolk were small in relation to Forestry Commission requirements as a whole, could not the Commission acquire all the land they want in one block say in a county such as Northumberland and leave the comparatively small areas of heathland remaining in Suffolk to be enjoyed in their natural state by the public? He felt that once the areas were planted up with regimented lines of conifers the general populace would lose all interest in the district (Forestry Commission archives, Santon Downham, uncatalogued)

Opposition to the forests has waned as the trees have matured, and current management policies are closely tailored to the needs of both conservation and recreation. The forests were badly damaged in the great gale of 1987, and replanting has taken place with these wider concerns, as much as the practicalities of timber production, firmly in mind.

Not all the twentieth-century woods in the Sandlings were deliberately planted. In a number of places, as we saw in Chapter Three, woodland has regenerated naturally across areas of neglected heathland: this woodland is dominated by birch and thorn, but in many cases includes a scatter of oak trees signalling the development of the final 'climax' vegetation. In addition, areas of wet 'carr' woodland, dominated by alder but with some willow and the occasional birch and oak, have grown up on lower ground where areas of fen have been neglected or grazed less intensively. Small areas of wet woodland have always existed in the district, often managed by coppicing, but their number and area increased significantly in the course of the late nineteenth and twentieth centuries.

Parks and pleasure grounds

Although, as we have seen, the Sandlings was an area dominated by large landed estates, great mansions and extensive gardens and parks are not a major component of its landscape. A number of small manor houses are, it is true, scattered across the district, with a particular concentration on the Shotley peninsula, including Shotley Hall, Erwarton Hall, and Stutton Hall. But the real 'stately homes' to which most of the land in the Sandlings was attached lay to the west, on the heavier soils of the boulder clay plateau. This was a pattern noted by Defoe in 1722, when he observed that there were 'some Gentlemen's Seats up further from the Sea, but very few upon the coast' (Defoe 1722, 54). The main reason for this distinctive pattern was probably that the claylands provided better opportunities for creating parks and pleasure grounds than the Sandlings itself. The heavy soils afforded better grass than the poor, bracken-filled sward of the sands; and, largely enclosed from a very early date, the clayland countryside contained more mature trees, woods and copses, all of which could be incorporated wholesale into parks and landscaped grounds. Whatever the explanation, most of the principal country houses in the area are located too far on to the clays to be considered, in any meaningful way, a part of the *Sandlings* landscape – places like Campsea Ashe, or Rendlesham. Nevertheless, two great eighteenth- and nineteenth-century residences, Benacre and Henham, lay at or close to the junction of sand and clay and just within the area of the modern AONB; and one, Sudbourne, lay entirely within the main area of the sands.

In addition to these, there was by the end of the eighteenth century a tight cluster of mansions, with large designed landscapes, along the Orwell estuary, including Orwell Park and Woolverstone, as well as a number on the Shotley peninsula. In part this concentration reflects the proximity of Ipswich, a fashionable social centre in the eighteenth century:

> There is a great deal of very good company in this town; and although there are not so many gentry here as at Bury, yet there are more here than in any other town in the county … (Defoe 1722, 46).

But equally important were the locality's natural beauties, the undulating countryside and the fine views across the Stour and Orwell estuaries. Eighteenth- and nineteenth-century visitors and commentators repeatedly praised the diversified scenery here. In 1867 the *Gardener's Chronicle*, describing Woolverstone, typically enthused that it was:

FIGURE 50.
A view in Tunstall Forest. The largest areas of woodland in the Sandlings are the Forestry Commission conifer plantations, established in the first half of the twentieth century.

> Impossible to convey by description any true idea of the grandeur of the views: there are five grand openings to the Orwell, which open out the best points on the river nearly the entire distance from Ipswich to Harwich … The whole of the opposite side of the river … is nearly an uninterrupted line of wood and park scenery. The fine seat of George Tomline, Esq. of Orwell Park, is right opposite Woolverstone; further

down the river is Broke Hall embossomed in sheltering woods and
presenting a pretty front towards the river (*Gardeners Chronicle* 1867, 157)

Sandlands

Designed landscapes before the nineteenth century

Before the middle decades of the eighteenth century country houses were
surrounded by highly artificial, geometric grounds. Gardens were enclosed by
walls or hedges and featured parterres – formal arrangements of grass, gravel
and planting – and displays of topiary. Such designs became ever more elaborate over time, culminating, in the decades either side of 1700, in the large
and complex grounds of the kind illustrated in 1707 by Kip and Knyff at
Brightwell, just outside the area of the AONB, only scant traces of which
remain on the ground today (Figure 51). More survives at Stutton Hall on the
Shotley peninsula, where Sir Edmund Jermy built a large mansion in 1553. A
contemporary garden enclosure still adjoins the hall to the north, its walls
featuring piers surmounted by finials, similar in design to the chimneys of the
house itself. An elaborate gate is set in the centre of the north wall, likewise
ornamented with finials. Its outer entrance – on the north side – has a low,
three-centre 'perpendicular' arch of normal Tudor form. The inside doorway,
however, facing the house, has a round classical arch with flanking fluted
pilasters (Figure 52). Not far away lies Erwarton Hall. A map of 1770 shows
the house surrounded by enclosed gardens and other courts, approached by an
avenue, and with fish ponds and a dovehouse in close proximity (IRO HE3
424). Earthwork traces of the ponds still survive, but the finest remaining
feature of the site is again a gateway, a massive affair, erected in *c.* 1550, with
round angle buttresses, pinnacles, and tunnel-vaulted archway.

In the sixteenth, seventeenth and eighteenth centuries some of the greatest
residences had deer parks in close proximity, areas similar to but normally less
densely wooded than the old medieval wood-pastures like Staverton. That at
Benacre was probably created in the seventeenth century and is shown on a
map of 1778. The park proper, a substantial rectangular area around the hall,
was divided into a number of sections, and an external pale embraced several
small fields, normal agricultural land, to the north (IRO T631 (rolls)). Rather
similar was the deer park at Henham, created by the Rous family in the
sixteenth century and shown on a fine map of 1699 (IRO HA 11 C9/19/2). This
again was divided into separate enclosures but here the hall, surrounded by its
enclosed gardens, was approached by a number of avenues – a kind of
geometric planting which became especially popular in the last decades of the
seventeenth century (Thomas 2003, 205–6). Both these parks, as already
noted, largely lay on clay soils on the fringes of the Sandlings, but Sudbourne
lay entirely on sand. It was probably created at the start of the seventeenth
century, soon after the estate was acquired by John Stanhope, for Norden's
map of 1601 seems to show its perimeter pale only partially completed, and a
public road still running through its centre (IRO EE5/11/1). Hodskinson's map
of Suffolk, published in 1783, shows three avenues fanning out northwards

from the house, two of which still survive. That running to the north-west consists of beech trees, mostly mid nineteenth-century in date, but featuring some apparently original specimens, with girths reaching 5.5 metres, at its southern end. Remains of a second avenue, ranged north–south, survive in the woodland to the north of the house. This is composed of limes, again mainly nineteenth-century but including at least two older specimens. Avenues were not restricted to parks. In the early eighteenth century a magnificent avenue of clumped beech trees was planted on the roadside, approaching Butley Priory, probably shortly after the gatehouse was converted into a residence in 1737 (Figure 53).

The second half of the eighteenth century saw three crucial developments in landscape design. Formal, geometric gardens were swept away from the walls of mansions; avenues and other geometric plantings became unfashionable and were often felled; and parks – now often without deer, and more open and aesthetic in character – became the prime setting for large houses. Additionally,

FIGURE 51.
Brightwell Hall and its gardens, as depicted in Johannes Kip and Leonard Knyff's *Britannia Illustrata* of 1707.

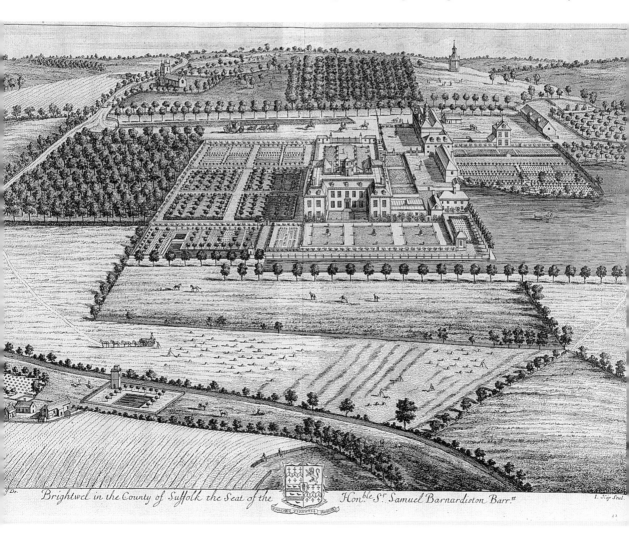

Brightwel in the County of Suffolk the Seat of the Hon.ble S.r Samuel Barnardiston Barr.tt

FIGURE 52.
The sixteenth-century
garden gate at Stutton
Hall.

the number of parks increased in this period, so that most landowners of any significance came to possess one (Jacques 1983; Williamson 1995). This fashion for setting the mansion within an open, 'naturalistic' landscape of grass and scattered trees, and placing gardens and pleasure grounds to one side of the main façade, is usually attributed to Capability Brown, but it was in fact part of a wider and more gradual development in which many designers played a part. Brown himself did not work on any of the parks in the Sandlings but another noted designer, Nathaniel Richmond, was probably responsible for the landscape created around the new house at Woolverstone, built for William Berners around 1776 by the architect John Johnson, although the evidence is circumstantial (Brown 1999; Williamson 2000, 67–8). If Richmond was indeed responsible, not all contemporaries were complimentary about his work. The

French tourist Francois de la Rochefoucauld described Woolverstone in 1784 as having 'an immense ill-kept park', consisting of 'a large expanse of enclosed ground artlessly covered with turf and trees' (Scarfe 1988a, 127). The Woolverstone Tithe Award map of 1839 (IRO FDA 298/A1/1b) – the earliest surviving map of the park – shows that it was indeed full of free-standing trees and small clumps, with larger areas of woodland to the south-east of the house and along the foreshore of the Orwell estuary. Circuitous carriage drives ran, in typical Richmond style, all through it. By this time an obelisk had been erected (in 1793) a short distance from the hall. The park went through many alterations in the nineteenth and twentieth centuries, and not much of the eighteenth-century landscape survives, although some of the oaks and sweet chestnuts in the north of the park may have been planted by Richmond; the sweet chestnut was one of his most favoured trees.

Orwell Park, on the opposite side of the estuary, was created soon after 1757, when John Vernon rebuilt the house there as a grand seven-bay Georgian mansion (IRO 119 50/3), but numerous additions and alterations were made to the design in the course of the eighteenth and nineteenth centuries. The park is now in divided ownership, and that section closest to the house – now a school – is largely occupied by playing fields. But the western portion

contains many fine oak trees, some apparently predating the creation of the park itself, and house and park still make a considerable impact upon the local landscape.

FIGURE 54.
above and opposite
Extract from Humphry Repton's Red Book for Broke Hall, Nacton, showing the proposed improvements to the view towards the Orwell.

Not only were entirely new parks laid out in the middle and later decades of the eighteenth century. Existing deer parks were also extensively modified in order to create something more fashionable. At Benacre the old park was expanded, and the main road diverted to the west, in the 1780s, in order to provide a more suitable setting for a new house, built by Sir Thomas Gooch (Bishop of Norwich and Ely), partly to designs by the Norwich architect Matthew Brettingham. Long entrance drives ran in from lodges positioned on the new public road (IRO FDA 24/A1/1b). The old internal subdivisions were removed and the park liberally planted with free-standing trees and clumps. At Henham, similarly, the old compartmentalised park was modernised in the second half of the eighteenth century (Thomas 2003, 211–13); and then more thoroughly reworked, this time by the famous designer Humphry Repton.

Repton was a native of Suffolk and carried out a number of commissions in the county. He prepared one of his 'Red Books' – an illustrated design proposal – for Henham in 1791. The Rous family's ancient courtyard house had burnt down in 1773, but it was another eighteen years before Sir John Rous began to erect a replacement, designed by the important country house architect James Wyatt, some 100 yards to the south, on a site probably chosen by Repton himself (Mackley 1996; Williamson 2000, 98–100). Repton suggested that a section of the old southern avenue, which was composed of limes, should be used to line part of a new south drive: the rest was to be

removed and a more 'modern' park laid out, with irregular scatters of trees and a number of clumps. The south entrance was to be supplied with a fine new lodge, flanked by plantations, and nearby farm buildings rebuilt in more 'picturesque' form. Brown and many other eighteenth-century designers had liked to mark the park off clearly from the surrounding countryside with a fairly solid perimeter belt of trees, but Repton was less keen on this kind of arrangement, instead preferring to open the peripheral woods at intervals in order to allow carefully selected views into the surrounding countryside. He proposed cutting a wide opening to the east of Henham Hall to open a vista towards the busy, distant port of Southwold. Many, but not all, of Repton's proposals seem to have been implemented, although the landscape we see here today has gone through many subsequent changes.

Repton was also employed at Wherstead, although little is known of his work there. But the 'Red Book' which he prepared in 1792 for Phillip Bowes Brook of Broke Hall at Nacton still survives (private collection; Williamson 2000, 103–4). Here again Repton worked in close association with the architect James Wyatt, who remodelled the hall in 1791–93. Repton was particularly concerned that the status of the mansion, and therefore the 'Dignity due to the long establishment of the Bowes family', was compromised by the fact that it adjoined the more extensive landscape of Orwell Park, and much of his design involved careful planting to obscure views of this neighbouring demesne. But Repton was also concerned to provide the mansion with a more 'cheerful' setting. The park was to be expanded and new plantations established, some positioned in such a way as to hide any views of the mudflats exposed in the Orwell estuary at low water and yet at the same time 'leave the channel beyond at all times open to the view' (Figure 54). Repton was enthusiastic about Wyatt's choice of the new 'Gothic stile' for the repairs and alterations to the house. It allowed him to retain the existing approach, along an old lime avenue to the west, for such an archaic feature would be 'perfectly consistent' with the gothic character of the house.

Nineteenth-century gardens and parks

Although in many ways Repton worked in the same broad style as earlier designers like Brown or Richmond, he was thus less hostile to formal elements like avenues, and in the later stages of his career he began to reintroduce terraces and other structural elements in front of the main façade of the house, and to create increasingly elaborate gardens (Daniels 1999). This trend continued and intensified after his death in 1816 and by the 1840s and 50s designers were laying out particularly extensive gardens which included many of the features – terraces, topiary, parterres – which had been fashionable in the seventeenth and early eighteenth centuries, before the vogue for 'nature' and informality (Elliott 1986). The change in taste was associated in part with a growing fashion for houses built in archaic 'gothic' styles, or in imitation of Italian Baroque mansions; and in part with a burgeoning interest in horticulture and plant collecting. Bedding-out schemes were increasingly popular, with plants like geraniums and pelargoniums used to create colourful and complex displays. A series of plans in the Suffolk Record Office thus records the development of the planting in the parterre beds at Broke Hall from 1844 to 1854. As well as the customary pelargoniums, other plants including verbenas, lobelias and salvia patens were employed, together with a range of bulbs – 'tulip of sorts', hyacinths and crocuses (IRO HA 61: 436/1,4; HA 93/3/250, 251, 252).

In the early 1850s William Andrews Nesfield, the most important and successful mid nineteenth-century gardener, provided designs for the gardens at Henham which featured an elaborate formal parterre to the south of the hall (Ridgeway 1993; IRO HA 11: C46/25 and 31). In an accompanying text Nesfield described how:

> When the character of the Park scenery immediately in front of the house is taken into account, it is obvious that the present monotonous and bald foreground is very objectionable, whereas a Parterre of ample dimensions would not only remedy this striking defect in a most cheerful manner (especially in winter without flowers) but would by the contrast of formality improve the distant scenery (IRO HA 11: C46/28)

Nesfield also altered the grounds of Orwell Park, at the same time as the house itself was extensively modified by the architect William Burn, with whom he often collaborated (Kenworthy Brown *et al.* 1981, 255); as well as those at Woolverstone. Here he again created a more formal and geometric setting for the house, which featured a broad parterre, terraces, central fountain, balustrades and urns laid out immediately in front of the north façade (*Gardeners Chronicle* 1867, 156–8). Beyond, also enclosed by a balustrade, accompanied by a substantial ha-ha and featuring two transverse terraces, was an extensive pleasure ground, stretching down towards the shore of the Orwell estuary. Unfortunately, only the outlines of the hard landscaping survive, in what is now the grounds of a private school.

Nesfield's expansion of the pleasure grounds and gardens at Woolverstone was accompanied by changes to the wider landscape, including, in particular, the creation of a new drive which provided a more imposing approach to the mansion from the direction of Ipswich. It led through a great western extension to the park, laid out in the 1850s. This is now a distinct property, physically separate from Woolverstone, under different ownership, and with its own name – 'Freston Park'. But it was never in reality a separate park (Williamson 2000, 137). In the 1560s the Latimer or Latymer family erected the romantic brick prospect tower which still survives here beside their manor house – even in the sixteenth century the view across the Orwell estuary was evidently considered an appealing one. By the early eighteenth century, however, the site had declined in status and was simply known as Hall Farm or Tower Farm. Some time before 1795 the estate was acquired by Charles Berners of Woolverstone, and a map of that date shows the hall and tower set within a purely agricultural landscape of enclosed fields, with areas of alder carr and marsh along the banks of the river Orwell (IRO HD 475/1819). Soon after 1850 a substantial part of the farm was laid to grass, the hedges removed, and many new trees planted. The new western drive, over three kilometres long, passed through the area from end to end, terminating at a new lodge, the 'Monkey Lodge', on the Ipswich Road. It was lined with copper beech trees, many of which still survive, and provided striking views across the picturesque Orwell estuary, as well as fine prospects towards Freston Tower. 'Freston Park' still survives under grass, with a number of fine trees. The attention paid to the park as well as to the gardens at Woolverstone was typical. In most parks in the Sandlings the planting was elaborated in the course of the nineteenth century, with much use of exotic conifers like the Wellingtonia (*Sequoia gigantea*). The number of drives was usually increased, and entrance lodges proliferated.

Designed landscapes after *c.*1880

The taste for elaborate, formal gardens continued into the early twentieth century, in the Sandlings as elsewhere. At Sudbourne, for example, a sales catalogue from 1905 describes the Lower Terrace with 'Gravelled Walks and Wide Lawns; and, on the right, a Rosery enclosed by forty-two brick piers ... and having in the centre a playing fountain; while, on the left, is a Shrub garden enclosed by a shaped Yew Hedge'. There were rock and water gardens, 'constructed of Tufa stone, with a comprehensive collection of Alpine Plants and rare Shrubs'. But on the whole there was now less money around to make improvements, or indeed to maintain what already existed, as the agricultural recession led to declining farm profits and thus to lower rental income for great landowners, problems that were particularly acute on the poor soils of the Sandlings. Only a few entirely new designed landscapes of any size were created in the district in this period, and usually by wealthy businessmen rather than established landowners. They began to feature a number of new elements, derived from the 'arts and crafts' style pioneered by designers like Edward Lutyens and Gertrude Jekyll (Williamson 2000, 156–60).

By the nineteenth century Stutton Hall had become no more than a working farm, and in 1887 it was purchased by James Oliver Fison, the agricultural chemical manufacturer (Williamson 2000, 163). He restored and extended the house, repaired its ancient garden walls and laid out fine new gardens in an 'arts and crafts' style to the south of the house, featuring lawns, topiaried yews and compartments defined by neat yew hedges, much of which survives in fine condition. But more striking was the new parkland which Fison created. The Ordnance Survey First Edition six inch map of 1884 shows an area of unadorned farmland to the north of the hall. By 1905 however, when the Second Edition six inch map was surveyed, a landscape park covering some 45 hectares had been created. This was, and still is, approached from the north by a long, straight drive, flanked by belts containing Scots and Corsican pine, horse and sweet chestnut, sycamore, oak and beech. Similar belts define the northern edge of the park, which was itself planted up in lively fashion with a mixture of oak, horse chestnut, sweet chestnut, Wellingtonia and (most striking of all) cedars – Cedar of Lebanon, Deodar cedar, and a number of examples of Atlas *glauca*. The result is an original and striking piece of landscape design, one of the last areas of private parkland to be created in East Anglia.

More striking still, however, are the house and grounds at Bawdsey Manor, which occupy an exposed coastal location immediately to the north of the Deben estuary. The house was the creation of Sir Cuthbert Quilter, a wealthy local businessman. Bawdsey began life in the 1880s as a small holiday home but it was expanded in stages to form the Quilter family's main residence, in a curious mixture of styles – gothic, Elizabethan, and Jacobean. Quilter built up a substantial estate in the area, and acquired the title of Lord of the Manor of Bawdsey. Like the house, the gardens were in a medley of styles, but their idiosyncratic character was also determined by the peculiar qualities of the site. In the words of the *Gardener's Chronicle* for December 1908, local conditions were 'absolutely opposed to the growth of all but the very hardiest species of plant'. The local winds were 'often sufficient to blow a plant out of the earth altogether'. Shelter was thus of supreme importance in the garden's design: so too was an emphasis on the more hardy alpines (*Gardener's Chronicle* December 1908, 406–9).

Quilter's mansion and its grounds still survive in degraded condition, bearing the scars of their subsequent use as an experimental radar station during the Second World War (below, pages 148–9). Immediately below the

FIGURE 55.
Bawdsey Manor:
Cuthbert Quilter's
artificial cliff.

house, to the south-west, is a series of red brick terraces, with a substantial boathouse built into the lowest level and an elaborate tea house on the top terrace, in a vaguely Jacobean style. The main area of gardens lies to the north-east and includes a circular rose garden, formed 'on the exact site of an old coastguard station [i.e., a martello tower], which he first had to blow up with explosives' (*Gardener's Chronicle* 1908, 408). This is connected to other parts of the grounds by a number of grotto-like underground tunnels. One leads to Bawdsey's most striking feature, the 'rockery wall' or artificial cliff, 50 metres high and extending along the shore for some 400 metres, constructed of cement generously embedded with artificial 'Pulhamite' stone and local crag (Figure 55). A precipitous path still leads along the side of the cliff, threading in and out of alcoves and cave-like recesses. Other features of the site included a cliff-top walk, lined with yews; a 'Pergola Garden' (Figure 56); and a kitchen garden which covers around two acres, complete with an orangery of wood

FIGURE 56.
Bawdsey Manor: the
Pergola Garden.

and glass. All of these features survive, albeit in ruined condition. Beyond the
gardens there were parkland grounds of *c.* 150 acres, occupied by grass lawns
and plantations, featuring in particular pines, holm oak, sweet chestnut and
sycamore.

In the course of the twentieth century a great house and extensive grounds
ceased to be the *sine qua non* of political power or the only real marker of
status, and as maintenance costs soared parks and mansions supported by
estates on such poor, marginal land were especially vulnerable. There was a
rash of post-War demolitions. Sudbourne Hall was knocked down in 1953 and
its park ploughed: only overgrown and degraded remains of the pleasure
grounds survive, together with some of the service buildings. Rendlesham
Hall, just outside the area of the AONB, went in 1949 and little remains of
its gardens and park, although many clumps and belts survive, together with
two unusual lodges. Henham was demolished in the 1950s but, somewhat curiously, its park remains under grass in surprisingly good condition, and much
of it is open to the public (Figure 57).

Other large houses have survived demolition. Woolverstone and Orwell
Park, both schools, and Broke Hall in Nacton, now divided into apartments,

FIGURE 57.
Ancient oak tree at
Henham, a relic of the
sixteenth-century deer
park.

are surrounded by the degraded remnants of their designed landscapes. Perhaps the most striking survivor is Benacre, where the imposing late eighteenth-century house, recently converted into upmarket apartments, stands within a magnificent park, packed with historical interest, which contains many ancient oak trees inherited from the earlier farming landscape.

Parks and pleasure grounds are thus not a significant feature of the Sandlings landscape, except in limited areas, but woodland makes a major impact almost everywhere and it comes as something of a surprise to learn that the overwhelming majority is so recent in date. As late as 1856 Glyde bemoaned the rather dull character of the scenery on the coast between Landguard Point and Dunwich, 'bleak and dreary, destitute of wood'. In the space of a century and a half – and in many place, much less than this – the character of the landscape has been transformed.

CHAPTER SIX

The Landscape of the Coast

·······

The dynamic coast

The coast itself – cliffs, beaches, shingle banks, the restless sea – probably makes a greater impression on visitors to the Sandlings than any other aspect of the landscape, even the heaths. The sea has also provided sustenance and employment for the local population, in the form of trade, ship-building, fishing and tourism, and has thus had a fundamental influence on the growth and morphology of the principal towns of Aldeburgh, Orford and Southwold, as well as of fishing villages like Walberswick. In addition, the Sandlings' coastal location also ensured that the district was at the front line in times of foreign wars, and the needs of defence have also left a significant mark. In all these and other ways, the sea has always been a key influence on the development of the landscape.

The Sandlings coast is a complex and dynamic environment, constantly experiencing both erosion and deposition. The soft rocks – London clay, crags and glacial drift deposits – are easily eroded by the sea, and as a result the coast has been evened out into a series of gentle, sweeping curves, or straight lines – features shared with much of the East Anglian coastline. Gentle promontories, rather than rocky headlands, are the characteristic landforms on coasts of this kind (Rackham 1986, 376–7; Steers 1969; Steers 1925). In the words of Glyde, 'the coast extends in a line tolerably regular' (Glyde 1856, 2).

The Sandlings thus boasts some of the most dramatic examples of coastal erosion in the country. A number of settlements have disappeared entirely, most notably the village of Easton Bavents, even its attached parish reduced, by the nineteenth century, to a narrow sliver of land. One phase in this process is recorded in the accounts of John Hopton, who owned the manor in the late fifteenth century. In 1475–76 the rent of the tenement held by one John Wiseman was reduced by 2d because part of it had fallen into the sea, and in the following year further reductions were made because a another 7½ acres (c. 3 hectares) had been eroded. Parts of the manorial demesne were also being eaten away: between 1464 and 1465 one piece of land, 4½ acres in extent, was reduced by an acre (Reinke 1999, 10–11). The neighbouring parishes have likewise suffered severe erosion, notably Covehithe, where the road today runs past the half-ruined church and a small cluster of houses, and then straight over the cliff (Figure 58). Whitaker, writing in the late nineteenth century, reported that the cliffs at Easton Bavents had retreated by 20 feet (*c.* 6 metres) in six years, while at Covehithe 84 feet (*c.* 26 metres) had been lost in the same period (Wheeler 1902, 25). Comparison of eighteenth-, nineteenth- and twentieth-century maps leaves no doubt that the coast here has indeed retreated to a very considerable extent (Figure 59). But the most famous example of coastal erosion is Dunwich, the ancient town where St Felix established the first bishopric of East Anglia in the seventh century. This has now been almost entirely washed away, the coast having retreated by nearly a quarter of a mile since 1587, to judge from a map surveyed in that year. Dunwich is probably the largest settlement in England to have been destroyed by the sea. With the erosion of Dunwich to its south, and of Easton Bavents to its north, Southwold ceased to be located within a shallow bay – Sole Bay – and became instead a slight promontory. The final stages in this process occurred relatively recently, as the bay was still recognisable enough to give its name to a great naval battle with the Dutch in 1672. The slight cape on which Southwold stands is still, somewhat mysteriously, labelled 'Sole Bay' on modern maps.

While there is thus no doubt that certain sections of the Sandlings coast have been eroding at a relatively rapid rate in the past, the scale of this process should not be exaggerated. Erosion is largely restricted to certain stretches of the coastline: from Dunwich south as far as Aldeburgh; and from Southwold north to Benacre. Elsewhere – as discussed below – the coast is, for the most part, accreting rather than eroding. The material removed from the soft cliffs is redeposited as spits of sand and shingle, behind which new land is gradually formed. Moreover, coastal erosion appears, to some extent, to be an episodic rather than a continuous process. Phases of rapid retreat have normally been followed by long periods of stasis, and the main factor determining rates of erosion was perhaps not the constant but slow pounding of the sea, but short-term phases of climatic deterioration – periods of storms and surges – such as that which occurred in the fourteenth century. The *Nonarum Inquisitiones* of 1341 records that 2,120 acres (858 hectares) of arable land had recently been lost in twelve coastal villages in Suffolk, together with 80 acres (32 hectares) of marsh in Aldeburgh (Bailey 1991, 192). The town of Aldeburgh is a classic case of such episodic retreat (Figure 60). A map of 1591 shows, in the main part of the town, three parallel streets lying back from the beach (IRO HD11/475 Aldeburgh). A survey of 1787, however, shows only two streets surviving, and the market place and the Moot Hall, which had earlier stood in the centre of the town, now standing beside the beach (IRO Isaac Johnson Collection HD11/475). This remarkable advance of the sea seems to have occurred in the second half of the seventeenth century. Yet very little has changed since. The present plan of the town is more or less identical to that shown on the 1787 map.

Human intervention might also have a significant impact on erosion rates. It has been suggested that the conversion of Southwold from shallow

FIGURE 58.
The coast at Covehithe is eroding rapidly: the road today runs past the half-ruined church and a small cluster of houses, and then straight over the cliff.

embayment to slight promontory – and its survival, in contrast to Dunwich's disappearance – was the consequence of the relative economic fortunes of the two places. Dunwich's haven in the mouth of the Dunwich river, immediately to the north of the city, became blocked by shingle and as a result the port declined in late medieval times but Southwold, with the mouth of the larger river Blyth remaining open, continued to flourish and could therefore afford to harden its defences (Rackham 1986, 377).

Wave action – 'longshore drift' – combined with strong north-easterly winds move the sand and shingle eroded from cliffs along the coast in a southerly direction, creating spits and ridges which grow and alter gradually over time. The most impressive and dramatic example is Orford Ness, sixteen kilometres in length and, at its neck, no more than 100 metres wide. To judge from the available documentary and cartographic evidence the spit may have grown at a rate of around thirteen metres per year between the twelfth and the nineteenth century (Steers 1926; Carr 1969). The Ness appears to have reached, more or less, its present form by the seventeenth century, to judge from maps surveyed by John Norden and others. Some authorities suggest that its extent at this time may have been the result of recent, rapid growth, for a rather schematic map made at some point in the 1530s suggests that the Ness then terminated some way to the north, more or less level with the town of

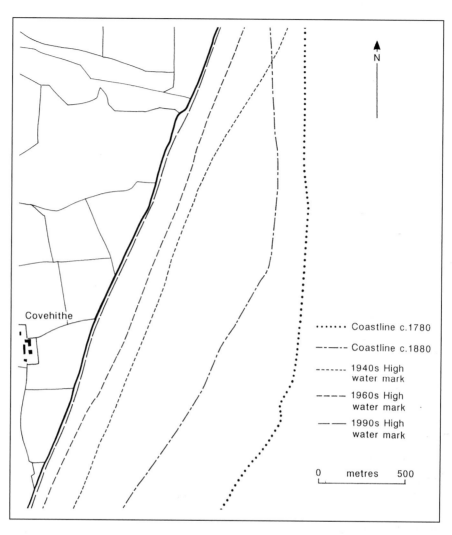

Coastline c.1780

Coastline c.1880

1940s High water mark

1960s High water mark

1990s High water mark

0   metres   500

FIGURE 59.
The changing coastline
at Covehithe (after
Hegarty and Newsome
2005).

Orford: but perhaps we should not put too much trust in such a source. Either way, the growth of this great spit has deflected the outfall of the river Alde southwards, allowing extensive salt marshes to form in its lea, mostly now reclaimed as grazing marsh. The river now turns abruptly southwards within a few metres of the sea and is obliged to run parallel with the coast before finally entering the sea at Shingle Street. Upstream from the point of deflection the river has been ponded back, creating a wide area of water and mudflats: an estuarine landscape lying, rather curiously, some way inland. Further north, constriction of the outfall of the Blyth by moving spits has similarly created the great inland marshes and mudflats of Bulcamp and Blythburgh.

The outfalls of the Alde and Blyth were deflected and constricted, but many lesser watercourses have had their exits to the sea completely blocked by shingle banks, their waters simply trickling through them to the sea or more recently – following post-medieval attempts at drainage and

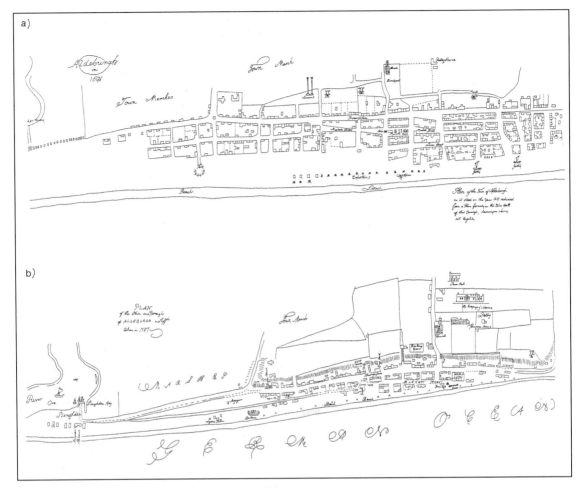

a)

b)

reclamation – passing through sluices. It was in such locations, as we have seen, that areas of peat fen often developed, many of which remained as damp commons until enclosure and drainage in the late eighteenth or early nineteenth centuries. In a few places, small lakes of fresh or brackish water also exist on the landward side of these obstructions – Benacre Broad, Covehithe Broad, Thorpness Mere – which represent, in effect, the relics of lost estuaries.

Ports and shipping

The absence of rocks, and the existence of long shingle beaches and sheltered estuaries, meant that the Sandlings coast was peculiarly attractive to seafarers from the earliest times. The wealth of the district in the Anglo-Saxon period was closely connected with the ease of communication offered by the sea. In the Middle Ages, too, the sea was crucial in the economic life of the area, for it was far cheaper to move heavy or indivisible cargoes by ship than by road.

FIGURE 60.
Rapid erosion at Aldeburgh. Top: a map, dated 1591, shows that there were at this time three streets in the town lying parallel to the beach. Below: by 1787, only two streets survived and the market place and the Moot Hall, which had earlier stood in the centre of the town, now stood beside the beach.

Sailors did face some problems, however. Coastal traffic used channels sheltered by sandbanks lying parallel with the coast, but these did not form a neat and continuous chain and crossing between and through them could be hazardous, especially at night or in poor weather, not least because their precise form and configuration were constantly changing. Moreover, even the friendliest shore could be a threat if the mariner was forced to make landfall unexpectedly or out of control, and in attempting to understand coastal landscapes like this we need to appreciate how they were viewed from the sea (Parker 2001, 32–3). Low-lying, featureless coasts can take a ship by surprise, and appropriate reference points are required to make it easier to 'read' from the sea. Landmarks might be erected to provide seafarers with aids to navigation, offering 'clearing lines or transits, alignments of nearer and further points in view which, when passed, permit a ship to turn in towards port or head off in another direction after passing a hazard' (Parker 2001, 35). The survival of Orford Castle is largely due to its importance in this respect. The government refused the Marquis of Hertford permission to demolish the tall keep in 1809 because, in the words of the *Suffolk Traveller* of 1829, it was 'a necessary landmark, especially for ships coming from Holland, which by steering so as to make the castle hide or cover the church, avoid a dangerous sand bank, called the Whiting' (Kirby 1829, 159). Landmarks often took the form of chapels or hermitages, some of which might serve as watch-houses or maintain beacons at night. It is possible that the chapel of St Margaret in Minsmere, in the parish of Leiston, was maintained in order to serve such a function long after Leiston Abbey was moved to a new site. It is also possible that the needs of mariners, as much as community pride, may explain the extraordinary height of many late medieval church towers in coastal parishes like Southwold, Walberswick or Covehithe. Some at least of the families and individuals who funded their construction derived their wealth from the sea. When, in 1686, a visitation determined that the tower of Alderton Church should be reduced in height because of decay, the incumbent appealed to Trinity House on the grounds that it was a seamark (Lingwood 1975). The tower of Hollesley church was similarly described in the early nineteenth century as 'a good flint structure and a useful sea-mark' (Kirby 1829, 137).

John Norden's drawing of Orford Castle, on the edge of one of his maps of the Stanhope estates, surveyed in 1600–01, shows a beacon blazing on the top of the keep, presumably as an aid to navigation (IRO EE5/11/1) (Figure 61). A few decades later, in 1634, Sir John Meldrum was granted permission to erect on nearby Orford Ness 'two temporary lighthouses to lead between Sizewell Bank and Aldeburgh Napes to the north', permission which he sold on, almost immediately, to one Gerard Gore (Long 1983, 53–7). The latter erected the first of a series of 'high' and 'low' lights on the Ness, mostly timber structures, which when viewed in alignment provided a safe passage through the gap between the two sandbanks (Long 1983, 57–74; Welch 1958). The 'high' masonry light built by Lord Braybrooke in 1792 was left as the sole light in

CASTRI ORFORDENSIS IN

1889, when the last of the 'low' lights was swept away. Trinity House, now in overall charge of coastal navigation, replaced the latter with a lighthouse built far to the north, in Southwold, and shipping then used bearings taken from these two lights, and from other floating lights, to navigate its way through a variety of offshore obstacles. Both Orford Ness light, and that at Southwold, still survive, the latter in particular – over thirty metres high and painted white – an icon of the Suffolk coast (Figure 62).

The most important medieval ports were at Dunwich, Aldeburgh, Southwold and Orford and, outside the boundaries of the AONB, Woodbridge, Felixstowe and Ipswich; but many other settlements, such as Blythburgh or Walberswick, had landing places for boats. All served significant trading functions, receiving goods both from the continent and from other parts of England, and exporting the produce of their agricultural hinterlands. But equally important were their fishing fleets. Domesday Book records that Dunwich paid an annual render of no fewer than 60,000 herring, Southwold 25,000, Blythburgh 3,000 and even Kessingland 10,000 (Campbell 2002). In the later medieval centuries Dunwich, Southwold and Aldeburgh were the main centres of the fishing industry but Walberswick, Thorpe and Sizewell also had significant fleets (Bailey 1990b).

FIGURE 61.
Orford Castle, as shown on John Norden's survey of the Stanhope estates, 1600–01. Note the beacon attached to the top of the keep, probably as an aid to maritime navigation.

The fate of these places, both in the Middle Ages and after, was intimately connected with the instability of the coast – with patterns of erosion and deposition. Movement of spits could seal estuaries or lead to pronounced silting, cutting communities off from access to the sea. Blythburgh was quite a significant port in the early Middle Ages, with a substantial fishery, but by the sixteenth century was badly affected by the silting of the Blyth. Frostenden lies several kilometres inland but its Domesday entry records that there was 'always one port' there: presumably the stream flowing into Easton Broad was at that time a tidal estuary (Morley and Cooper 1922). Thirteenth-century documents in the cartulary of Butley Priory describe the mouths of the Kessingland, Benacre, Dunwich and Minsmere Rivers, as well as that of the Hundred River to the north of Aldeburgh, as still open to the sea and used as havens for boats. Even in the seventeenth century some of these estuaries remained open. The anonymous author of the *Chorography of Suffolk*, writing in 1605, described how 'At Yoxford springs a little river [i.e., the Minsmere River] that floweth to Fordley and to Theberton ... and so directly into the sea where it maketh the haven called Minsmere haven' (MacCulloch 1976, 21).

The town of Orford was founded by Henry II in the 1160s, as described

FIGURE 62.
The lighthouse at Southwold, erected in 1890.

above (page 100), beside the new castle which he erected there. The open sea was originally close to the town, for Orford Ness had not as yet grown as far south as today: Orford was a port lying near the mouth of a sheltered haven. Broad Street and Daphne Road, which run just below the five metre contour, may follow close to the line of its original quay. The southward growth of Orford Ness and the accumulation of mudflats and salt marsh in its lea ensured that the town was gradually marooned some distance inland, as its quay migrated towards the river, while at the same time the approach from the open sea, along the Ore, became longer and more difficult. In 1586 Camden was able to describe Orford as 'once a large and populous town, forti-fy'd with a Castle of reddish stone ... But now it complains of the Sea's ingratitude, which withdraws it self by little and little, and begins to envy it the advantage of a harbour' (Camden 1695, 374). By 1722 Defoe could write that the place was 'once a good town, but is decayed, and as it stands on the land-side of the river, the sea daily throws up more land to it, and falls off itself from it, as if it was resolved to disown the place, and that it should be a sea port no longer' (Defoe 1722, 54).

Erosion was also a threat to the prosperity of the ports. The most striking example is unquestionably Dunwich. In the twelfth century this town rivalled Ipswich. All that survives today are its western, suburban fringes, including the wall and gateway of the Franciscan friary and the Romanesque leper-chapel dedicated to St James, located, like most leper-houses, beyond the city ramparts. Dunwich was minting coins in the tenth century and was therefore already, in all probability, defended. By the thirteenth century it had eight (possibly nine) parish churches, several religious houses, and a number of market places (Scarfe 1986, 129–37). The sea's advance was gradual but relent-less. Already by the time of Domesday one carucate (120 fiscal acres) of land had been lost to the sea. The church founded by St Felix in the seventh century disappeared at an early date; St Leonard's church was washed away around 1300. In 1328 storms choked the harbour with shingle and diverted the mouth of the Dunwich River northwards, and by 1350 more than 400 houses, together with shops and windmills, were said to have been destroyed. Shortly afterwards the churches of St Bartholomew, St Michael and St Nicholas fell into the waves. The church of St John, which stood beside the Great Market, was dismantled around 1540 to save its materials from tumbling over the cliff. In 1570 the town's South Gate and Gilden Gate were destroyed, but the church of St Peter's was still standing in 1700 when, like St John's, it too was dismantled (Scarfe 1986, 129–37) (Figure 63).

By the sixteenth century the most important ports along the Sandlings coast were Southwold and Aldeburgh (together with Woodbridge, Ipswich and Felixstowe outside the AONB), although trade continued at many other places, including Walberswick and Dunwich (although the submerged ruins here made the approach unsafe for boats). All benefited from the agrarian wealth of their hinterland, sending wheat, barley, malt and dairy produce to London and elsewhere. The most important import was unquestionably coal, brought from the north-east of England. Aldeburgh was now the pre-eminent port, directly benefiting from the decline of Dunwich: it became a borough in 1547 (Allen 1982; Crook 1982; Clodd 1959). Camden described in 1586 how its harbour was 'very commodious for mariners and fishermen, by which means the place is populous, and is much favour'd by the Sea, which is a little unkind to other towns upon this coast' (Camden 1695, 374). In the Middle Ages ships visiting Aldeburgh had mainly harboured in Thorpe Haven or Almouth, to the north of the town, the outlet for the Hundred River, but this was becoming blocked by shingle by the start of the sixteenth century. Maritime activity was then concentrated to the south of the town, on the river Alde at Slaughden, situated on the landward side of the great spit of Orford Ness and thus reached by a long passage up the river Alde. A new quay was built here between 1542 and 1575, and this became a thriving ship-building area, as well as an important fishery and port (Allen 1982; Clodd 1959, 80–2). Grain and malt were exported, together with apples, bacon, hemp, leather, cloth and salt, mainly to London: and a variety of goods were imported from the Continent, including salt and grain, as well as coal from the north-east (Allen 1982). The town's prosperity is reflected in the size of its church and also in its picturesque timber-framed moot hall, constructed in the early sixteenth century (Figure 64). Southwold also prospered in the fifteenth and sixteenth centuries, as the size of its magnificent church testifies. Its principal harbour lay to the south of the town, on the river Blyth. Lesser landing places at Walberswick and, by this time, Dunwich, were also reached through the narrow entrance to the river, which then widened out into a broad and complex 'inland estuary':

> S'woul and Dunwich and Walberswick
> All go in at one lousy creek (Defoe 1722, 55)

Coastal trade remained important into the seventeenth and early eighteenth centuries, although it now grew more slowly. Additionally, the local fishing fleets were badly affected by competition from the Netherlands, and several of the small ports went into decline. John Kirby in 1764 described Walberswick as 'formerly a large place which traded considerably with the sea, but now is very mean'. But traffic increased again from the middle of the eighteenth century, a period in which the economy of the agricultural hinterlands was particularly buoyant (Lawrence 1990, 5). Not all the ports benefited to the same extent, however, with Aldeburgh – which suffered, as we have seen, from drastic erosion in the later seventeenth century – now going into a relative decline.

The Sandling's long rivers ensured that goods could be moved by water far inland, once transhipped at coastal ports into smaller craft, principally keels and wherries. From Aldeburgh, such craft could negotiate the upper reaches of the Alde as far as Iken and Snape Bridge, where substantial maltings were erected in the middle of the nineteenth century. In the 1880s White's *Directory* was able to describe the 'commodious wharf, up to which

FIGURE 63.
Aerial view of
Dunwich: only the
western margins of the
medieval town,
including the remains
of the Franciscan friary,
now survive.

the Alde is navigable for vessels of 100 tons burthen. From 25,000 to 30,000 quarters of malt are shipped yearly for London and other markets ...' (White 1885, 627). The Blyth, in contrast, was by the mid eighteenth century only navigable by commercial craft as far as Blythburgh Bridge. In 1757 the River Blyth Navigation Act was passed, and improvements commenced to make the river navigable as far upstream as Halesworth (HA 85:3116/480). This initiative followed hard on improvements made to the harbour at Southwold, which included the construction, in 1749 and 1752, of two piers at the mouth of the Blyth, to reduce the speed with which it became blocked by shingle

(Kirby 1829, 204–5). The navigation scheme, led by the Halesworth brewer Thomas Knights, was initially successful (Lawrence 1990; Boyes and Russell 1977, 98–107). Four locks and a tidal staunch were constructed, Blythburgh bridge was rebuilt and raised, and a small quay built at Halesworth. Goods were transhipped from sea-going ships onto smaller wherries at Reydon or at Blackshore, near Southwold, and by the 1830s over 60 per cent of the coal shipped through Southwold Harbour was destined for Halesworth. But a combination of factors led to the navigation's decline. There were continuing problems with the build-up of shingle banks across the mouth of Southwold harbour. Indeed, large-scale reclamation of the wetlands bordering the Blyth creek in the later eighteenth and early nineteenth century had made the situation worse by reducing the amount of water flowing through the mouth of the Blyth at each tide, and thus the extent to which the harbour entrance was scoured. It was calculated in 1840 that 1,504 acres had been reclaimed on the margins of the creek, reducing the volume of water leaving and entering on each tide by more than 148 million cubic feet (Boyes and Russell 1977, 106–7). Between 1805 and 1818 the harbour mouth had to be dug out thirteen times and in 1839 the outlet was impassable for some time (Boyes and Russell 1977, 106–7). But economic factors also played their part in the decline of the navigation. All over England the viability of canals and other waterways was being challenged by the expansion of the rail network. The 1850s, 60s and 70s saw a steady decline in the volume of trade along the Blyth, and in 1884 the Commissioners announced that the income from tolls was insufficient to keep the locks and bridges in repair. The Navigation was, however, sporadically used until 1911, and only officially closed in 1934 (Boyes and Russell 1977, 107).

The natural problems constantly experienced by the various coastal harbours were likewise exacerbated by economic factors, primarily the continuing improvements made to terrestrial transport, which made investment in facilities for coastal shipping less and less attractive. Throughout the later eighteenth and nineteenth centuries proposals were made to remedy the difficulties caused by shifting banks and accumulating shallows, but sufficient investment was never forthcoming. Some schemes were particularly ambitious, such as that proposed in the 1830s for creating a large new harbour at the mouth of the river Orwell, a project which would have involved the construction of locks in the channel called The Gull, to the west of Halvergate Island, in order to form a reservoir of 80 acres, the release of waters from which would have scoured the harbour entrance (IRO HA 65 4/5: Wise 1836). More practical were the various plans for a new harbour at Aldeburgh. In 1783 the Earl of Aldborough bemoaned the condition of the port and the fact that the approach from Orford Haven was particularly difficult and winding. He noted that 'there are a great number of seamen nearby starving for want of employment' and urged that a new dock and shipyard should be constructed on the shore (IRO HD1064/1). Plans were also put forward on a number of occasions in the nineteenth century for making direct sea access to Slaughden (IRO HD83/2/76; HA11/B7/7–9). In 1872 a parliamentary act was actually passed to create such a harbour, in spite of an engineer's report which argued persuasively that it would soon become blocked with sand, and a petition drawn up by landowners in the nearby Iken Level protesting that the proposed change would increase the dangers of flooding there (IRO HA5: 50/10/3.3 and 3.4). But in the event the scheme was abandoned.

Only Felixstowe, at the extreme south of the Sandlings, and Ipswich, just outside the district to the west, are now major ports. Ipswich grew in importance due to a series of improvements in the early nineteenth century, culminating in the opening of what was then the largest docks in Britain, if not the world (Malster 1999). Felixstowe saw considerable development of its infrastructure in the late nineteenth century thanks to the activities of Colonel George Tomline, who instigated the construction of a new railway line from Ipswich in 1877 and the construction of the new docks in 1881, completed in 1884 at a cost of £101,000 (Rouse 1982; IRO HD21: 360/70–74). It failed to develop economically, however, until the establishment of the container port here in the 1960s, which is now a vast and successful enterprise. The other Sandlings ports have declined slowly through the nineteenth and twentieth centuries as their harbours silted, the size of commercial ships gradually increased, and the importance of coastal trade declined in the face of competition from the railways. Industrial Felixstowe and Ipswich lie firmly outside the boundaries of the designated Area of Outstanding Natural Beauty: Southwold, Orford and Aldeburgh are firmly within it, exuding that tranquillity of faded glory that contributes so much to the district's distinctive character.

Landscapes of leisure: holiday resorts

Some declining coastal settlements found other ways of making a living. By the late eighteenth century, if not before, the wealthier members of society were beginning to appreciate the healthy air and relaxation provided by a sea-side sojourn. In 1829 it was reported that:

> Aldeburgh, depopulated and impoverished by the encroachments of the sea was, till within the last 20 years, hastening to complete decay; but several families of distinction, wishing for a greater degree of privacy and retirement than can generally be found at a fashionable watering-place, having made this town their summer residence ... Instead of the clay-built cottages of the poor, which impressed the mind with a gloomy feeling of dirt and misery being hid within, we now see many neat and tasteful mansions ... (Kirby 1829, 147)

There is still a notable concentration of fine Georgian residences on the cliff top above the town. And Aldeburgh was not alone: the same source reported how Southwold 'has for several years past been the resort of strangers who visit the sea-coast during the summer season' (Kirby 1829, 205–6). Yet while the wealthy might build fashionable summer residences on the coast, or take up seaside lodgings for the season, it was only in the second half of the nineteenth century that large-scale tourism took off, and the familiar landscape of sea-side resorts – featuring hotels, boarding houses, piers, golf links, promenades and the rest – began to appear along the coasts of England. This development was fuelled by higher levels of disposable income among the burgeoning middle classes and, in particular, by the arrival of the railways (Walton 1983). In the words of one writer, 'the railways turned dozens of obscure ... seaside villages into holiday resorts within an incredibly short time' (Lindley 1973, 15). In some parts of England, most notably the south coast, major developments were occurring by the middle decades of the nineteenth century, but in the Sandlings it was only in the 1870s and 80s that the holiday industry really got under way.

A branch line was constructed from Saxmundham to Aldeburgh in 1860. This was primarily intended to serve Garrett's engineering works at Leiston and the small fishing industry at Aldeburgh itself, but it also served to stimulate the local tourist trade. In the late 1870s work began on building a pier in the town, part of the mania for these things that swept England after the passing of the General Pier and Harbour Act of 1861 made it easier for

consortia of businessmen and local authorities to undertake their construction (Rouse 1982; IRO AE150/8/8.3–8.6). The Aldeburgh pier was only ever half-finished, however, and was eventually abandoned altogether and demolished: Aldeburgh remained, and remains, a very small resort. Southwold, further north, was more successful. Here, too, the arrival of the railways in 1879 was a spur to the development of tourism. In this case, however, the branch from Halesworth took an idiosyncratic form – a narrow-gauge line, run by an independent company, which itself became something of a tourist attraction. In 1889 the *Cliff Hotel* was constructed by the brewers Adnams, followed by the *Marlborough* in 1900 and the *Grand* in 1901 (Rouse 1982, 77–8). In 1900, as part of a particularly late flurry of pier-building activity, the town acquired a pier, one of the last to be built in the country and – like those constructed at Lowestoft and Felixstowe – the work of the Coast Development Company, founded in 1898. It carried a small pavilion but served principally as a place to land passengers brought by steamers from London (Rouse 1982, 77–8).

Felixstowe, outside the AONB, also flourished in the late nineteenth century as a resort, following the construction of the new railway line from Ipswich. As well as the new docks, two new hotels were built, the *Pier* and the

FIGURE 65.
The early twentieth-century holiday village at Thorpness: timber-framed and weatherboarded houses overlook The Meare.

FIGURE 66.
Thorpeness: the 'House in the Clouds'.

Manor House (Rouse 1982, 48–50). West Carnie, writing in 1898, remarked how 'the houses are scattered about here, there and everywhere, over a huge area' (Carnie 1899, 85–6). In 1902 the Felixstowe and Walton Improvement Act gave the Council the authority to acquire land along the sea front and construct a sea wall with two miles of promenade (Rouse 1982, 50–1).

Probably the most idiosyncratic resort on the Suffolk coast is Thorpness. In 1898 Thorpe, in the parish of Aldringham, was described as 'a quaint little hamlet on the Suffolk coast. If ever a place gave the impression of being dropped from the clouds, that place is Thorpe … There is no street and only one shop' (Carnie 1899, 55). Five years later the place was inherited by Glencairn Stuart Ogilvie, barrister and dramatist, and in 1910 the site, suitably renamed, began to be developed as a holiday village, catering for the wealthy middle class. Its central feature was a twenty-five hectare lake developed from the natural mere which had, like others on the coast, formed behind a coastal spit. Around this were scattered neat houses decorated with timber-framing and weatherboarding – a kind of idealised suburbia, magically transported to the seaside (Figure 65). In 1914 a new station was opened on the Saxmundham-Aldeburgh line to serve the resort and, while development of the site was interrupted by the outbreak of the First World War, it resumed soon after its close (Rouse 1982, 124–7). Curiosities of the village include an early nineteenth-century post mill which was moved here from nearby Aldringham and used to pump water into an unusual water tower, the 'House in the Clouds', in which the water tank itself is disguised as a house, perched on top of the tall, weather boarded tower (Figure 66).

A number of holiday resorts thus developed along the Sandlings coast in the late nineteenth and early twentieth centuries, but all are small, rather genteel places. The district never saw the development of the kind of huge, sprawling holiday settlements which characterise, for example, parts of the coast of Sussex, Hampshire, or Lancashire. It was, and to some extent still is, remote from major centres of population and the principal resorts were only ever served by branch lines. Paradoxically, their failure to expand has ensured that Southwold and Aldeburgh, in particular, retain a lively if discrete holiday industry. In the second half of the twentieth century cheap air travel achieved on an international scale what, in the previous century, railways had done on a national one, and many of England's larger resorts have experienced serious economic decline in the face of foreign competition. But the appeal of these places, which seem little more than enlarged fishing villages, remains strong in this heritage-conscious age, as local house prices so clearly testify.

Landscapes of defence: before the twentieth century

Coasts were important for defence, as well as for trade, fishing and leisure. This is especially true of the Sandling's coast, facing towards Europe, with its low cliffs, an absence of rocks and reefs, and miles of gentle, inviting beach. Hollesley Bay and Sole Bay, because they provided sheltered anchorages, were of particular strategic significance, and a gun battery was constructed at Dunwich as early as 1479 (Gardner 1754, 179). Harwich Haven was of even greater importance in this respect as it offered the best deep-water harbour on the East Anglian coast, and was thus widely seen as offering a potential back door to London for foreign attackers. In 1539, worried about the possibility of an invasion from France and the Holy Roman Empire, Henry VIII ordered the construction of a number of defences along the south and east coast which included 'bulwarkes of earth and wood' on Landguard Point at the mouth of the Haven. These were dismantled in 1552 but were restored in 1588 when the Spanish Armada threatened; new batteries were built at the same time at Southwold and Aldeburgh. After a period of neglect all three of these defences were upgraded in the seventeenth century, and it was at this time (in 1625) that the first true fort was constructed on Landguard Point, with four bastions, brick barracks and turf ramparts (Kent 1988, 99–110).

The eighteenth century saw further developments. Landguard Fort was demolished and rebuilt in 1717; while in 1744, during the War of the Austrian Succession, new batteries were established at Aldeburgh and Southwold – the latter still surviving, much restored, on Gun Hill (Kent 1988, 110, 153) (Figure 67). Landguard Fort was again rebuilt, now with five bastions, and complex earthworks were added during the American War of Independence. But it was the threat of French invasion, during the Napoleonic Wars, which produced the most comprehensive system of coastal defences seen so far along the Sandlings coast. The batteries at Aldeburgh and Southwold were maintained, and the fort at Landguard again modified; floating batteries were installed in the mouths of the Deben and the Alde; and, most important of all, a number of Martello towers were constructed along the southern stretch of the Sandlings coast (Sutcliffe 1972; Kent 1988, 21–2, 91–5).

The primary purpose of these squat circular towers – named after a similar construction at Mortella in Sicily, which had successfully repulsed a seaborne attack by the Royal Navy – was to protect the coast from ships armed with heavy guns. A total of 105 were erected along the southern and eastern coasts of England, of which 47 survive. The earliest towers were constructed between 1805 and 1808 in Kent and Sussex; these were followed by a series of slightly larger examples built along the coasts of Essex and Suffolk, as far north as Aldeburgh, between 1808 and 1812. There were seventeen in all along the Suffolk coast, of which ten remain today (Sutcliffe 1972).

The towers are about ten metres high, and built of brick which was externally rendered and lined to resemble ashlar masonry (Figure 68). Each had two floors and a heavy gun mounted on the top, protected by a parapet 1.8 metres thick. There were many variations in detail. Most were protected by dry moats, for example, but that at Walton Ferry also had a wet ditch. The tower erected at Slaughden Quay in Aldeburgh, the most northerly of the series, was exceptional. It carried four guns and had a quatrefoil plan, resembling four 'normal' towers interlocking (Figure 69). Most of the towers

were built close to sea level, protecting exposed beaches from enemy landing. But a few were on higher ground, overlooking the mouths of estuaries or other strategic points. Six towers (two with batteries) were thus built fairly close together between Shingle Street and the north of Bawdsey, defending the inviting beach of Hollesley Bay. To the south, the high mud cliffs of Bawdsey meant there was no need of towers until the mouth of the Deben was reached: entry to this strategically important watercourse was defended on the north by a tower and battery on high ground, near what is now Bawdsey manor, and to the south by towers (some of which are still extant) and a battery in the north of Felixstowe parish. South of this, there is another short gap in the sequence, again corresponding with a run of cliffs, followed by another series of four towers which protected the beaches at Felixstowe, and then others – at Landguard Point, Shotley, and Trimley – guarding the entrance to Harwich Haven and the mouths of the rivers Stour and Orwell.

Other defences were added to the coast in the later nineteenth century. A seven-sided fort with fourteen guns was built on Shotley Point in 1862, and yet further rebuildings of, and alterations to, Landguard Fort were carried out in the early 1870s, 1888 and 1898 (Kent 1988, 124–8). The fort, now in the care of English Heritage, represents one of the most important post-medieval

FIGURE 67.
Gun Hill, Southwold: the six eighteen-pounder guns were first placed here in 1744.

FIGURE 68.
opposite above
A typical martello tower near East Lane, Bawdsey.

FIGURE 69.
opposite below
The martello tower at Slaughden, just south of Aldeburgh, is the most northerly in the series, the largest, and is built to an unusual quatrefoil plan.

military sites in the country (Figure 70). It incorporates parts of the early eighteenth-century fort, and more substantial remains from the rebuilding of 1745–50, but the visible structures largely date to the various reconstructions of the late nineteenth century, in particular the great curving granite casemated gun battery overlooking the river, and the substantial semi-circular barrack block.

Landscapes of defence: the twentieth century

The First World War has left little trace in the local landscape, although there was a strong military presence in the district, which included Royal National Air Service landing grounds at Aldeburgh and Covehithe and various coastal lookouts, including one in the Martello tower at Aldeburgh. But the threat of German invasion at the start of the Second World War had a sudden, dramatic and to some extent enduring impact (Newsome 2003). A scarcity of resources in the wake of the disaster at Dunkirk ensured that emphasis was placed on England's first line of defence – its beaches. Sudbourne Hall and Benacre Hall were occupied by the military, and the villages of Iken and Sudbourne were evacuated. Aerial photographs taken by the RAF both during and immediately after the War show the vast extent of the defence works, which were planned by the Royal Engineers but constructed, for the most part, by local contractors. There was, by late 1940, 'an almost continuous band of anti-invasion defences stretching from beyond the county's northern boundary near Lowestoft down to the most southerly part of the Suffolk coast proper, Landguard Point' (Newsome 2003, 46). These included pillboxes, gun batteries and emplacements, concrete anti-tank blocks, anti-tank and anti-glider ditches, lengths of scaffolding on the beaches, and mile upon mile of barbed wire. Defence was concentrated in the same general areas as the earlier Martello towers, on the more inviting beaches and around the mouths of the principal estuaries. Indeed, some Martello towers (as at East Lane, Bawdsey and Aldeburgh) were reused as pillboxes or observation posts (Newsome 2003, 49). But in addition there were particularly strong defences around Bawdsey Manor, which was occupied by the military as an experimental station in 1937 and which was, in consequence, bombed no less than twelve times during the course of the War. It was here that Robert Watson-Watt and his team developed the new and immensely important military technology of radar (Kinsey 1983). The four giant transmitter masts, each 360 feet high, have gone (the last was removed in 2000) but underground bunkers and the transmitter block (currently under restoration, thanks to the Bawdsey Radar Group) remain, together with numerous pillboxes and gun emplacements built into Cuthbert Quilter's artificial cliffs.

Inland, there were major air bases at Leiston and at Bentwaters, opened in 1943 and 1944 respectively and used by the USAF; and at Woodbridge, which was opened in 1942 to accommodate returning aircraft which were badly damaged, low on fuel, or otherwise in need of an emergency landing place

(Bowyer 1990, 59–60, 142, 218–21). To cater for such crippled craft it was equipped with a particularly large runway, 3,000 yards long and 250 yards wide, the construction of which necessitated the felling of more than a million young trees planted in the previous decade by the Forestry Commission (Bowyer 1992, 219).

Most of the coastal defences were removed at the end of the War – some had gone even before this. The long lines of scaffolding and barbed wire, and the minefields at Shingle Street and around Thorpness and Aldeburgh, have left no trace. But large numbers of pillboxes remain within the area of the AONB (Figure 71). The majority are hexagonal in plan (FW3/22 and 3/24 types) but there are also scattered examples of square and octagonal forms, and many idiosyncratic variants, especially in the area around Bawdsey Hall, where they are densely packed (Wills 1985). Numerous examples of the concrete cubes designed to stop enemy tanks can also be found. Other remains from this important phase of the Sandling's history are rather less obvious, like the anti-glider trenches which can still be traced at Church Walks in Sudbourne, or beside the Anglo-Saxon burial mounds at Sutton Hoo (Figure 8). At a number of places – as at Barthorp's Creek in Hollesley – existing drainage dykes were widened to provide anti-tank defences (Newsome 2003, 49); while the entire area of drained marshland to the south of Walberswick was deliberately flooded in order to slow down an enemy advance, and never again reclaimed.

Military involvement in the area did not end with the coming of peace in 1945. Landguard Fort was occupied by the army until 1956; the airfields at Bentwaters and Woodbridge continued to be operated by the USAF into the 1990s. Above all, in this Cold War world, the long, lonely promontory of Orford Ness was developed as a testing ground for the Atomic Weapons Research Establishment and the Royal Aircraft Establishment. The site already had a history of military experimental use, having been used by the Royal Flying Corps as a research station as early as 1915, and it was here that Watson-Watt undertook his first experiments in the use of radar between 1935 and 1937, before he and his team moved to Bawdsey Manor (Kinsey 1981). But it is the grim archaeology of the Cold War that distinguishes the site, now in the care of the National Trust. The most impressive structures are the 'Pagodas', with their huge concrete roofs designed to absorb accidental explosions – not from a nuclear bomb, but from the conventional charge associated with the delivery device, while this was being tested to ensure that it was robust enough to withstand the various pressure it would experience during delivery. These curious, sinister structures seem peculiarly at home in this bleak and lonely setting, striking monuments to this most frightening phase of Britain's history (Figure 72).

FIGURE 70.
opposite
Landguard Fort, at the mouth of Harwich Haven, has a long and complex structural history, but the visible remains date mainly from the later nineteenth century.

FIGURE 71.
A typical Second World War pillbox at Bawdsey.

FIGURE 72.
One of the sinister 'pagodas' on the Orford Ness nuclear testing range.

CHAPTER SEVEN

Postscript

The countryside of the 'Suffolk Coast and Heaths' has probably changed more than that of any other specially designated landscape in England – Area of Outstanding Natural Beauty, or National Park – in the course of the last century and a half. In 1850 there would have been more hedges and hedgerow trees but, above all, far less woodland, and far more heath. As we have seen, the dramatic transformation in the landscape during this period is almost entirely due to changes in the economics and technology of agriculture. But in all periods the landscape of the Sandlands was primarily moulded by purely practical and economic activities, by people farming, fishing, or otherwise making a living. We now wish to conserve its distinctive features for rather different reasons – for their aesthetic value, their importance for wildlife conservation or tourism. Buildings and structures rendered redundant by technological or economic change have accordingly acquired new roles, instead of being swept away: most strikingly, perhaps, the vast industrial complex at Snape Maltings, which now provides a fine concert hall, shops, and other leisure and tourist facilities.

But new roles for the landscape bring new challenges, and conservation involves careful management and a careful balancing of the many and varied demands made upon the land. The district is less well known, perhaps, than most other 'designated' areas in Britain. It does not attract such vast hordes of visitors as The Lake District or the Peak District. But it does suffer to some extent from the problems which always result when inherited beauty is given special protection. House prices are high by local standards and the summer months bring serious over-crowding and congestion to places like Southwold, Walberswick or Aldeburgh. But away from such limited 'hot spots' the landscape, even at the height of the summer, is surprisingly tranquil. Heaths, marshes and coast still exude a strangely lonely, melancholic atmosphere, one in which the most striking twentieth-century contribution to the landscape – Sizewell nuclear power station – seems, like the 'Pagodas' at Orford Ness, curiously at home. The landscape is also surprisingly wild and 'natural' in appearance. Indeed, it is the wide reed beds, woods and the expanses of heather that draw most visitors to the district, especially bird-watchers, rather than its more obviously historical or 'cultural' aspects. And yet, as should by now be very apparent, little in this 'Area of Outstanding Natural Beauty' is in any meaningful sense 'natural'. Everything has been shaped by the hand of man, and much that we see today gained its appearance in very recent times.

Postscript   Yet at the same time the influence of nature *is* everywhere apparent, in the particular character of the raw materials which were available to be transformed by successive societies: in the poor sandy soils, for example, which gave rise to the heaths, the great conifer plantations, even the particular patterns of ownership which have shaped so much of the district's history. Above all it is manifest in the sea, arguably the most important influence on the local landscape: pounding the soft cliffs at places like Dunwich or Covehithe; steadily, inexorably moving the sand and shingle to block estuaries and deflect streams and rivers. Reading the documents and maps relating to the history of the Sandlings ports and navigation, and of reclamation and sea defence, I have been struck again and again by how vulnerable, puny and defenceless local communities have always been in the face of the immense and unpredictable power of the sea. The fortunes of individuals, and of places, have always been shaped by this most unremitting of nature's forces: and they still are. In the twenty-first century we can, admittedly with difficulty, protect this precious landscape from unrestrained or unsympathetic development, and can give it new roles in tourism, the leisure industry, and wildlife conservation. But defending it from the sea is a challenge on an altogether different scale. If, as seems likely, global warming continues, and sea levels rise significantly, the influence of the sea on lives and landscapes in the Sandlings will increase. Then hard choices will have to be made about which parts of this fragile coastline, and its distinctive cultural and natural heritage, we protect, and which we abandon to the waves.

Bibliography

Allen, M. (1982) *The Development of the Borough of Aldeburgh 1547–1660: Aspects of the Economy of the Borough*, unpublished MA dissertation, University of Wales at Aberystwyth.

Allen, J., Potter, V. and Poulter, M. (2002) *The Building of Orford Castle: A Translation from the Pipe Rolls 1163–78*, Orford Museum, Orford.

Allison, K. J. (1957) 'The sheep-corn husbandry of Norfolk in the sixteenth and seventeenth centuries', *Agricultural History Review* **5**, 12–30.

Armstrong, P. (1973) 'Changes in the Suffolk Sandlings: a study of the disintegration of an eco-system', *Geography* **58**, 1–8.

Bailey, M. (1988) 'The rabbit and the medieval East Anglian economy', *Agricultural History Review* **36**, 1, 1–20.

Bailey, M. (1989) *A Marginal Economy? East Anglian Breckland in the Later Middle Ages*, Cambridge University Press, Cambridge.

Bailey, M. (1990a) 'Sand into gold: the evolution of the foldcourse system in west Suffolk, 1200–1600', *Agricultural History Review* **38**, 40–57.

Bailey, M. (1990b) 'Coastal fishing off south east Suffolk in the century after the Black Death', *Proceedings of the Suffolk Institute of Archaeology and History* **37**, 2, 102–14.

Bailey, M. (1991) 'Per impetum maris', in *Before the Black Death*, ed. B. Campbell, Manchester University Press, Manchester, 184–208.

Banks, S. J. (1988) 'Nineteenth-century scandal or twentieth-century model? A new look at open and close parishes', *Economic History Review* **41**, 51–73.

Barnes, G. and Williamson, T. (2006 in press) *Hedgerow History: Ecology, History and Landscape Character in Norfolk and Beyond*, Windgather Press, Macclesfield.

Beardall, C. and Casey, D. (1995) *Suffolk's Changing Countryside*, Suffolk Wildlife Trust, Ipswich.

Berlyn, A. (1898) *Sunrise-Land: Rambles in Eastern England*, London.

Blair, J. (1988) 'Minsters in the landscape', in *Anglo-Saxon Settlements*, ed. D. Hooke, Blackwells, Oxford, 35–58.

Blake, E. O. ed. (1962) *Liber Eliensis*, Camden Society, 3rd ser. **92**.

Bowyer, M. J. F. (1990) *Action Stations 1: Wartime Military Airfields of East Anglia, 1939–1945*, Patrick Stephens, Cambridge.

Boyes, J. and Russell, R. (1977) *The Canals of Eastern England*, David and Charles, Newton Abbot.

Brown, D. (1999) *One of the Gentleman Improvers: the Career of Nathaniel Richmond*, unpublished PhD thesis, University of East Anglia.

Brown, P. (1986) *Sibton Abbey Cartularies and Charters, Part 2*, Suffolk Record Society, Woodbridge.

Brown, P. (1987) *Sibton Abbey Cartularies and Charters, Part 3*, Suffolk Record Society, Woodbridge.

Brunskill, R. W. (1978) 'Distributions of building materials and some plan types in the domestic vernacular architecture of England and Wales', *Transactions of the Ancient Monument Society* **23**, 46–57.

Burrell, E. (1960) *An Historical Geography of the Sandlings before 1840*, unpublished MSc thesis, University of London.

Butcher, R. (1941) *The Land of Britain: Suffolk (East and West)*, Land Utilisation Survey, London.

Camden, J. trans. E. Gibson (1695) *Britannia*, Oxford.

Campbell, J. (2002) 'Domesday herrings', in *East Anglia's History: Studies in Honour of Norman Scarfe*, eds. C. Harper-Bill, C. Rawcliffe, and R. G. Wilson, Boydell, Ipswich, 5–17.

Carnie, West (1899) *In Quaint East Anglia*, Greening, London.

Carr, A. P. (1969) 'The growth of Orford Spit: cartographic and historical evidence from the sixteenth century', *Geographical Journal* **135**, 28–39.

Carver, M. (1992) 'The Anglo-Saxon cemetery at Sutton Hoo: an interim report', in *The Age of Sutton Hoo: The Seventh Century in North-western Europe*, ed. M. Carver, Boydell and Brewer, Woodbridge, 343–72.

Carver, M. (1998) *Sutton Hoo: Burial Ground of kings?*, British Museum Press, London.

Chatwin, C. P. (1961) *British Regional Geology: East Anglia and Adjoining* Areas, HMSO, London.

Clodd, H. P. (1959) *Aldeburgh: The History of an Ancient Borough*, Adlard, Ipswich.

Coleman, S. (1999) 'Crown post roofs', in *An Historical Atlas of Suffolk*, eds. D. Dymond and E. Martin, 3rd edn, Suffolk County Council, Ipswich, 178–9.

Coleman, S. and Barnard, M. (1999) 'Raised aisled halls and queen post roofs', in *An Historical Atlas of Suffolk*, eds. D. Dymond and E. Martin, 3rd edn, Suffolk County Council, Ipswich, 180–1.

Cotterill, J. (1993) 'Saxon raiding and the role of the late Roman coastal forts of Britain', *Britannia* **24**, 227–40.

Cramp, R. (1984) 'Iken cross-shaft', *Proceedings of the Suffolk Institute of Archaeology and History* **35**, **4**, 291–2.

Crook, J. M. (1982) *Two Suffolk Coastal Towns since the Early Middle Ages*, unpublished BSc dissertation, University of Nottingham.

Cunliffe, B. (1995) *Iron Age Britain*, Batsford, London.

Daniels, S. J. (1999) *Humphry Repton: Landscape Gardening and the Geography of Georgian England*, Yale University Press, London.

Darby, H. C. (1957) *The Domesday Geography of Eastern England*, Cambridge University Press, Cambridge.

Defoe, D. (1722) *A Tour through the Whole Island of Great Britain*, London.

Dickens, A. G. (1951) *The Register or Chronicle of Butley Priory, Suffolk, 1510–1535*, Warren, Winchester.

Dimbleby, G. W. (1962) *The Development of British Heathlands and their Soils*, Clarendon Press, Oxford.

Dolman, P. C. J. (1978) *Windmills in Suffolk: A Contemporary Survey*, Suffolk Mills Group, Drinkstone.

Dutt, W. A. (1901) *Highways and Byways in East Anglia*, Methuen, London.

Edwards, G. ed. (1991) *George Crabbe: Selected Poems*, Penguin, Harmondsworth.

Elliott, B. (1986) *Victorian Gardens*, Batsford, London.

Evans, N. (1999) 'People and poor in 1674', in *An Historical Atlas of Suffolk*, eds. D. Dymond and E. Martin, 3rd edn, Suffolk County Council, Ipswich, 96–7.

Eyre, S. R. (1955) 'The curving ploughland strip and its historical implications', *Agricultural History Review* **3**, 80–94.

Fairclough, J., and Plunkett, S. J. (2000) 'Drawings of Walton Castle and other monuments in Walton and Felixstowe', *Proceedings of the Suffolk Institute of Archaeology and History* **39**, **4**, 419–59.

Farrand, R. (2002) *Enclosure in the Sandlings*, unpublished MA dissertation, University of East Anglia.

Fenwick, V. (1984) 'Insula de Burgh: excavations at Burrow Hill, Butley, Suffolk, 1978–1981', in *Anglo-Saxon Studies in Archaeology and History*, vol 3, eds S. C. Hawkes, J. Campbell and D. Brown, 35–54.

Filmer-Sankey, W. and Pestell, T. (2001) 'Snape Anglo-Saxon Cemetery: excavations and surveys 1824–1992', *East Anglian Archaeology* **95**, Archaeological Service, Suffolk County Council, Ipswich.

Gardner, T. (1754) *An Historical Account of Dunwich*, London.

Glyde, J. (1856) *Suffolk in the Nineteenth Century: Physical, Social, Moral, Religious and Industrial*, Simpkin, London.

Hamerow, H. (1991) 'Settlement mobility and the 'Middle Saxon Shift': rural settlement patterns in Anglo-Saxon England', *Anglo-Saxon England* **20**, 1–17.

Hanley, J. A. (1949) *Progressive Farming*, 4 volumes, Caxton, London.

Hardy, M. and Martin, E. (1986) 'Archaeological fieldwork: South Elmham St Cross and South Elmham St James', *Proceedings of the Suffolk Institute of Archaeology and History* **36**, 147–9.

Hardy, M. and Martin, E. (1987) 'Archaeological fieldwork: South Elmham St Margaret, All Saints and St Nicholas', *Proceedings of the Suffolk Institute of Archaeology and History* **36**, 232–5.

Harper-Bill, C. ed. (1980) *Blythburgh Priory Cartulary Part One*, Suffolk Record Society, Woodbridge.

Harper-Bill, C. ed. (1981) *Blythburgh Priory Cartulary Part Two*, Suffolk Record Society, Woodbridge.

Haselgrove, C. (1982) 'Wealth, prestige and power: the dynamics of late Iron Age political centralisation in England', in *Ranking, Resource and Exchange: Aspects of the Archaeology of Early European Society*, eds. C. Renfrew and S. Shennan, Cambridge University Press, Cambridge, 282–96.

Haslam, J. (1992) '*Dommoc* and Dunwich: a reappraisal', *Anglo-Saxon Studies in Archaeology and History* **5**, 41–6.

Hegarty, C. and Newsome, S. (2005) *The Archaeology of the Suffolk Coast and Inter-Tidal Zone*, unpublished report for the National Mapping Programme, English Heritage and Suffolk County Council, Swindon.

Hervey, Lord F. ed. (1902) *Suffolk in the Seventeenth Century: The Breviary of Suffolk by Robert Reyce*, London.

Hodge, C., Burton, R., Corbett, W., Evans, R. and Scale, R. (1984) *Soils and their Use in Eastern England*, Soil Survey of England and Wales, Harpenden.

Holderness, B. A. (1972) '"Open" and "close" parishes in England in the eighteenth and nineteenth centuries', *Agricultural History Review* **20**, 126–39.

Hoppitt, R. (1992) *The Development of Deer Parks in Suffolk from the Eleventh to the Seventeenth Century*, unpublished PhD thesis, University of East Anglia.

Hoppitt, R. (1999) 'Rabbit warrens', in *An Historical Atlas of Suffolk*, eds. D. Dymond and E. Martin, 3rd edn, Suffolk County Council, Ipswich, 68–9.

Jacques, D. (1983) *Georgian Gardens: The Reign of Nature*, Thames and Hudson, London.

Johnson, C. J. (1980) 'The statistical limitations of hedge dating', *Local Historian* 14, 28–33.

Kent, P. (1988) *Fortifications of East Anglia*, Terrence Dalton, Lavenham.

Kenworthy-Browne, J., Reid, P., Sayer, M. and Watkin, D. (1981) *Burke's and Savill's Guide to Country Houses, Volume 3: East Anglia*, Burkes' Peerage, London.

Kerridge, E. (1967) *The Agricultural Revolution*, Allen and Unwin, London.

Kinsey, G. (1981) *Orfordness – Secret Site: A History of the Establishment 1915–80*, Terrence Dalton, Lavenham.

Kinsey, G. (1983) *Bawdsey – Birth of the Beam. The History of the RAF Stations at Bawdsey and Woodbridge*, Terrence Dalton, Lavenham.

Kirby, J. (1735) *The Suffolk Traveller*, 1st edn, London.

Kirby, J. (1764) *The Suffolk Traveller*, 2nd edn, London.

Kirby, J. (1829) *The Suffolk Traveller*, London.

Kneale, N. ed. (1973) *Ghost Stories of M. R. James*, Folio Soc., London.

Land Use Consultants (1993) *The Suffolk Coast and Heaths Landscape: A Landscape Assessment Prepared for the Countryside Commission, Suffolk County Council, Suffolk Coastal District Council* (etc), Land Use Consultants, Walgrave.

Land Use Consultants (1999) *National Research on Locally Distinctive Hedgerows*, Land Use Consultants/ Countryside Agency, London.

Lawrence, R. (1990) *Southwold River: Georgian Life in the Blyth Valley*, Moxon, Southwold.

Lawson, A. J., Martin, E. and Priddy, D. (1981) 'The Barrows of East Anglia', *East Anglian Archaeology* 12, Norfolk Archaeological Unit, Norwich.

Lewis, C., Mitchell-Fox, P. and Dyer, C. (2001) *Village, Hamlet and Field: Changing Medieval Settlements in Central England*, 2nd edn, Windgather Press, Macclesfield.

Lindley, K. (1973) *Seaside Architecture*, H. Evelyn, London.

Lingwood, H. R. (1975) 'Alderton's seamarks', *East Anglian Magazine* 24, 314–16.

Long, N. (1983) *Lights of East Anglia*, Terence Dalton, Lavenham.

Loveday, R. and Williamson, T. (1988) 'Rabbits or ritual? Artificial warrens and the Neolithic long mound tradition', *Archaeological Journal* 145, 290 – 313.

Lucy, S. (2000) *The Anglo-Saxon Way of Death: Burial Rites in Early England*, Suttons, Stroud.

MacCulloch, D. ed. (1976) *The Chorography of Suffolk*, Suffolk Record Society, Woodbridge.

Mackley, A. (1996) 'The construction of Henham Hall', *Georgian Group Journal* 6.

Malster, R. (1999) 'Navigation, ports and trade', in *An Historical Atlas of Suffolk*, eds. D. Dymond and E. Martin, 3rd edn, Suffolk County Council, Ipswich, 132–3.

Marshall, W. (1787) *The Rural Economy of Norfolk*, 2 vols, London.

Martin, E. (1988) 'Burgh: Iron Age and Roman enclosure', *East Anglian Archaeology* 40, Suffolk County Planning Department, Ipswich.

Martin, E. (1993) 'Settlements on hill-tops: seven prehistoric sites in Suffolk', *East Anglian Archaeology* 65, Suffolk County Planning Department, Ipswich.

Martin, E. (1999a) 'Suffolk in the Iron Age', in *Land of the Iceni: The Iron Age in Northern East Anglia*, eds J. Davies and T. Williamson, Centre of East Anglian Studies, Norwich, 45–99.

Martin, E. (1999b) 'Bronze Age Suffolk', in *An Historical Atlas of Suffolk*, eds. D. Dymond and E. Martin, 3rd edn, Suffolk County Council, Ipswich, 38–9.

Martin, E. (1999c) 'Medieval moats', in *An Historical Atlas of Suffolk*, eds. D. Dymond and E. Martin, 3rd edn, Suffolk County Council, Ipswich, 60–1.

Martin, E. (1999d) 'Hundreds and liberties', in *An Historical Atlas of Suffolk*, eds. D. Dymond and E. Martin, 3rd edn, Suffolk County Council, Ipswich, 26–7.

Martin, E. (2001) 'Rural settlement patterns in rural Suffolk', *Annual Report of the Medieval Settlement Research Group* 15, 5–7.

Matthews, G. V. T. (1969) 'Nacton Decoy and its catches', *Wildfowl* 20, 131–7.

Morley, C. and Cooper, E. R. (1922) 'The sea port of Frostenden', *Proceedings of the Suffolk Institute of Archaeology and History* 18, 167–79.

Mortimer, R. ed. (1979) *Leiston Abbey Cartulary and Butley Priory Charters*, Suffolk Record Society, Woodbridge.

New, A. S. B. (1985) *A Guide to the Abbeys of England and Wales*, Constable, London.

Newman, J. (1992) 'The late Roman and Anglo-Saxon settlement pattern in the Sandlings of Suffolk', in *The Age of Sutton Hoo: the seventh century in north-western*

Europe, ed. M. Carver, Boydell and Brewer, Woodbridge, 25–38.

Newman, J. (2000) 'Sutton Hoo before Raedwald', *Current Archaeology* **180**, 498–505.

Newsome, S. (2003) 'The coastal landscapes of Suffolk during the Second World War', *Landscapes* **4**, **2**, 42–58.

Newton, S. (1993) *The Origins of Beowulf and the Pre-Viking Kingdom of East Anglia*, Boydell and Brewer, Woodbridge.

Norden, J. (1618) *The Surveyor's Dialogue*, London.

Northeast, P. (1999) 'Religious houses', in *An Historical Atlas of Suffolk*, eds. D. Dymond and E. Martin, 3rd edn, Suffolk County Council, Ipswich, 70–1.

Parker, A. J. (2001) 'Maritime landscapes', *Landscapes* **2**, **1**, 122–41.

Payne Gallwey, Sir R. (1886) *The Book of Duck Decoys: their construction, management, and history*, London.

Peterken, G. F. (1968) 'The development of vegetation in Staverton Park', *Field Studies* **2**, 1–39.

Pevsner, N. (1974) *The Buildings of England: Suffolk*, Penguin, Harmondsworth.

Pollard, E., Hooper, M. D. and Moore, N. W. (1974) *Hedges*, Collins, London.

Postgate, M. R. (1973) 'Field systems of East Anglia', in *Studies of Field Systems in the British Isles*, eds. R. A. Baker and A. R. H. Butlin, Cambridge University Press, Cambridge, 281–324.

Rackham, O. (1976) *Trees and Woodlands in the British Landscape*, Dent, London.

Rackham, O. (1986) *The History of the Countryside*, Dent, London.

Rackham, O. (1999) 'Medieval Woods', in *An Historical Atlas of Suffolk*, eds. D. Dymond and E. Martin, 3rd edn, Suffolk County Council, Ipswich, 64–5.

Raynbird, W. and Raynbird, H. (1849) *On the Farming of Suffolk*, London.

Reeves, A. and Williamson, T. (2000) 'Marshes', in *The English Rural Landscape*, ed. J. Thirsk, Oxford University Press, Oxford, 150–66.

Reinke, G. (1999) *The Landscape History of the Sandlings Marshes: With Particular Reference to Benacre and Kessingland*, unpublished MA dissertation, University of East Anglia.

Ridgeway, C. (1993) 'William Andrews Nesfield: between Uvedale Price and Isembard Kingdom Brunel', *Journal of Garden History* **13**, 69–89.

Roberts, B. A. and Wrathmell, S. (2002) *Region and Place: A Study of English Rural Settlement*, English Heritage, London.

Robinson, D. H. (1949) *Fream's Elements of Agriculture*, 13th edn, John Murray, London.

Rodwell, J. S. (1991) *British Plant Communities Volume 2: Mires and Heaths*, Cambridge University Press, Cambridge.

Rouse, M. (1982) *Coastal Resorts of East Anglia*, Terrence Dalton, London.

Scarfe, N. (1986) *Suffolk in the Middle Ages*, Boydell and Brewer, Woodbridge.

Scarfe, N. ed. (1988a) *A Frenchman's Year in Suffolk: French Impressions of Suffolk Life in 1784*, Suffolk Records Society, Woodbridge.

Scarfe, N. (1988b) 'Domesday settlements and churches: the example of Colneis hundred', in *An Historical Atlas of Suffolk*, eds. D. Dymond and E. Martin, 1st edn, Suffolk County Council, Ipswich, 42–3.

Scarfe, N. (1999) 'Medieval and later markets', in *An Historical Atlas of Suffolk*, eds. D. Dymond and E. Martin, 3rd edn, Suffolk County Council, Ipswich, 76–7.

Scott, R. (2002) *Artists at Walberswick: East Anglian Interludes 1880–2000*, Art Dictionaries Ltd., Bristol.

Shirley-Price, L. and Latham, R. E. (1990) *Bede's History of the English Church and People*, Penguin, Harmondsworth.

Simper, R. (1967) *Over Snape Bridge: The Story of Snape Maltings*, Ipswich.

Skipper, K. and Williamson, T. (1997) *Thetford Forest: Making a Landscape, 1922–1997*, Centre of East Anglian Studies, Norwich.

Steers, J. A. (1925) 'Suffolk shore: Yarmouth to Aldeburgh', *Proceedings of the Suffolk Institute of Archaeology and History* **19**, 1–14.

Steers, J. A. (1926) 'Orford Ness: a study in coastal physiography', *Proceedings of the Geologists Association* **37**, 306–25.

Steers, J. A. (1969) *The Sea Coast*, Collins, London.

Sutcliffe, S. (1972) *Martello Towers*, David and Charles, Newton Abbot.

Swanton, M. ed. (1996) *The Anglo-Saxon Chronicle*, Dent, London.

Tate, W. E. and Turner, M. 1978. *A Domesday of English Enclosure Acts and Awards*, Reading.

Taylor, C. (2000) 'Fenlands', in *The English Rural Landscape*, ed. J. Thirsk, Oxford University Press, Oxford, 167–87.

Tennyson, J. (1939) *Suffolk Scene: A Book of Description and Adventure*, Blackie & Son Ltd, London.

Thomas, M. (2003) *Trees and Woodland in the Suffolk*

Landscape, unpublished PhD thesis, University of East Anglia.

Todd, H. and Dymond, D. (1999) 'Population densities, 1327 and 1524', in *An Historical Atlas of Suffolk*, eds D. Dymond and E. Martin, 3rd edn, Suffolk County Council, Ipswich, 80–3.

Trist, P. J. O. (1971) *A Survey of the Agriculture of Suffolk: Royal Agricultural Society of England County Agriculture Surveys No. 7*, Royal Agricultural Society, London.

Wade, K. (1993) 'The urbanisation of East Anglia: the Ipswich perspective', in 'Flatlands and Wetlands: Current Themes in East Anglian Archaeology', *East Anglian Archaeology* 50, ed. J. Gardiner, Scole Archaeological Committee, Norwich, 144–51.

Wade Martins, S. and Williamson, T. (1999) *Roots of Change: Farming and the Landscape in East Anglia 1700–1870*, Agricultural Society of Great Britain, Exeter.

Walton, J. K. (1983) *The English Seaside Resort: A Social History, 1750–1914*, Leicester University Press, Leicester.

Warner, P. (1996) *The Origins of Suffolk*, Manchester University Press, Manchester.

Warner, P. (2000) *Bloody Marsh: A Seventeenth-century Village in Crisis*, Windgather Press, Macclesfield.

Welch, C. E. (1958) 'Sir Eduard Turnour's lighthouses at Orford', *Proceedings of the Suffolk Institute of Archaeology and History* 28, 62–74.

Wentworth Day, J. (1979) 'Sudbourne, a Suffolk estate reborn', *East Anglian Magazine* 38, 12, 650–1.

Wentworth Day, J. (1981) 'The duck decoys of Suffolk', *East Anglian Magazine* 40, 122–25, 170–2.

West, S. (1984) 'Iken, St Botolph, and the coming of East Anglian Christianity', *Proceedings of the Suffolk Institute of Archaeology and History* 35, 4, 279–301.

Wheeler, W. H. (1902) *The Sea Coast*, London.

White, W. (1885) *History, Gazetteer and Directory of Suffolk*, London.

Whittaker, J. (1918) *British Duck Decoys of Today*, London.

Williamson, R. (1996) 'Southwold's sea-salt works', *Suffolk Review*, New Series 23, 23–26.

Williamson, T. (1995) *Polite Landscapes: Gardens and Society in Eighteenth-century England*, Sutton, Stroud.

Williamson, T. (2000) *Suffolk's Gardens and Parks: Designed Landscapes from the Tudors to the Victorians*, Windgather Press, Macclesfield.

Williamson, T. (2002) *Hedges and Walls*, National Trust, London.

Williamson, T. (2003) *Shaping Medieval Landscapes: Settlement, Society, Environment*, Windgather Press, Macclesfield.

Willmott, A. (1980) 'The woody species of hedge with special reference to age in Church Broughton parish, Derbyshire', *Journal of Ecology* 68, 269–286.

Wills, H. (1985) *Pillboxes: A Study of UK Defences, 1940*, Secker and Warburg, London.

Wise, C. (1836) *A Plan of the Proposed Harbour at Orfordness*, Ipswich.

Wymer, J. (1999) 'Surface geology', in *An Historical Atlas of Suffolk*, eds. D. Dymond and E. Martin, 1st edn, Suffolk County Council, Ipswich, 18–19.

Young, A. (1795) 'A fortnight's tour in East Suffolk', *Annals of Agriculture* 23, 38–40.

Young, A. (1797) *General View of the Agriculture of the County of Suffolk*, 1st edn, London.

Index

Page numbers in **bold** type refer to the figures